FITNESS BUSINESS MASTERY

The book *every* fitness
coach needs to read as
soon as they qualify

CHRIS BRADLEY

R^ethink

First published in Great Britain in 2023
by Rethink Press (www.rethinkpress.com)

Cover image © Shutterstock | Lenka Horavova and Lemonsoup14

Contents

Preface

I've written this book to be of value to you as a fitness business owner through the actionable content, honesty and transparency about the challenges of running your own fitness business. The story of how I got to this point won't be one you're familiar with, though, so hang tight for a laugh.

Up until two years ago, I had only read two books in my life, and the only reason I did was because I was forced to in school. They didn't interest me. But then again, nothing in school did except playing football or badminton. This showed in my literacy skills, teacher feedback and exam results. I made a valiant attempt at higher history – I liked learning about the wars – but my efforts got me to exam day and no further. The first question read, 'With the benefit of hindsight…' Did I know what hindsight meant? Absolutely not. I spent the remaining hour pretending to write and left the hall with my head hanging in shame.

After leaving school with minimal qualifications, the natural routes at the time were apprenticeships, college or the dole. I applied for a HNC (Higher National Certificate) in Sports Coaching at College in Glasgow, and was invited to attend the open day. At the time, I remember thinking how stressful it was. The 'advice' given by the school was that what you chose to do now was what you would do for the rest of your life so 'choose carefully'. This turned out to be nonsense, but you can imagine the fear it brought on.

I got to the college and they had merged the HNC and the HND (Higher National Diploma) together, HND being the longer course that required better results to join. As they talked through the course curriculum, I soon realised that everyone in the room was there for the HND. All the books they handed out had 'HND' on them. I thought, 'I've managed to blag my way in here.' I started to worry. Part of me didn't even want to be there anyway, as I was well out of my comfort zone.

When the lecturer showed around twelve of us around the campus, we walked out of the room in twos. I realised we were supposed to take our books with us, so I ran back to grab them and chucked them in my bag. As I walked back out the room, I saw my fellow students and the lecturer getting into the lift about 100 yards away. I figured they were probably getting the lift down to the first floor, so I scurried down the stairs after them. But when I looked around, I couldn't find them.

The action I took next will stay with me forever and quite frankly, it's a moment I've come back to in my mind many times since. After two or three minutes of searching, I left the building. At the time, it was an instinct, but now I'm sure it was because I was out of my depth. I was doing something totally out of my comfort zone and I'd looked for the first speed bump along the road to quit. I remember the huge sense of relief as I left. It was like I had escaped. That tells you everything you need to know. I went straight for a sausage roll, jumped on a bus and went back to tell my mum the fake news (more on my wee mum later). Our conversation went like this:

'How was it, son?'

'Uh, full of geeks and not what I thought it would be.'

'OK, son, their loss.'

The takeaway from that experience is glaringly obvious. Do I regret it? No, but how I handled it doesn't sit well with me. My question for you is this: have you had a moment like that in your life? Do you regret not taking *that* chance?

The rest of this section will make you feel better and will help you turn your mistake into a lesson. Fast-forward the clock. After six years working in retail and a few summers working in Ayia Napa drinking vodka that makes you see sounds, meeting amazing people and learning and growing as a person, it was time to knuckle down.

I qualified as a personal trainer in 2013 and started working in a gym a few months later while also working in the bookies. I kept the other job on until I picked up fitness clients, working twenty-five hours a week in the bookies, fifteen hours of shifts for the gym and then delivering PT sessions on top. But the hours weren't the hardest part. Going from a gym environment, with like-minded personal trainers and members who wanted to better themselves by getting fitter and healthier, to spending the next day sitting behind a bandit screen in the bookies full of cigarette butts and people absolutely hating life – that was the hard part.

It served as my motivation to get out, which was later fuelled by an incident over annual leave typical of a large retail company. I was preparing for my first professional photoshoot. I gave my line manager twelve weeks' notice that I needed a particular Sunday off. It came to two weeks before and they put me in to work the full day. 'Told you, couldn't promise you anything.'

I had kept the second job on far too long to be 'safe', but now I was done. My hand was forced, and I gained twenty-five hours back in my diary. This made me roll my sleeves up and not only replace the money I'd lost but make more. I started picking up more clients and eventually had a stacked one-to-one diary.

A year or so later, I hit a brick wall. I was working from 6am to 7pm in the gym six days a week. On top of that, I'd spend Saturday and Sunday making changes to clients' plans, booking them in and setting up new clients for the week ahead. I loved it, but passion only gets you so far. It started to feel like a house of cards. Any time I had weekend plans or a holiday, the guilt was always hanging over me, preventing me from fully enjoying myself.

You're a one-person band when you start your own business and the buck stops with you. That feeling slowly sucked the enjoyment out of the job. I got to a point where I just couldn't handle all the extra stuff that came with it – chasing up payments, dealing with cancellations, paying tax, overcoming quiet spells, sorting out tech complications, etc. So I applied for a role as Assistant Gym Manager. It was for less than my PT wage, but I was looking at the positives: consistent pay cheque, still in the fitness industry, managing a team – something I enjoyed – and the first step on a career ladder. Later I realised this was another example of me looking to bail instead of addressing challenges head on.

I didn't get the job – thankfully. It felt like a kick in the teeth at the time, but it might be my single biggest blessing ever, more so than running away from college. I didn't know it at the time, but instead of chasing another position, all I had to do was address the weakest parts of my business. Why was scheduling taking me so long? Why were some clients cancelling? Why was I having to chase payments?

It was up to me to answer those questions, but I didn't know that. I figured that out later, and I'm so glad I did. Many coaches fail because they don't get that knowledge. But you won't be one of them – everything I've learned since then is getting poured into this book for you.

Now I'm here servicing personal trainers and online coaches and awaiting a wedding date to marry the woman of my dreams. I'm incredibly chuffed and grateful for the position I'm in. And another reason I'm in this position? My mother. She raised me and my brothers Lee and Matthew, pretty much on her own. She gave us everything she possibly could. She's been my biggest inspiration since day one. Thanks, Mum, and sorry I lied to you the day I left college. I hope you'll be as happy/proud as I am about what I decided to do instead.

Introduction

How did you feel the day you got your Level 3 certificate? You probably fall into one of three camps that led you to that moment. You might have quit your 'safe' job to pursue a career in fitness, you might have decided to build up your training business while working a second job, or you might just love exercise and training so much that you figured, why not get paid for it?

Regardless of the scenario, it's likely that you qualified feeling ill-prepared for the challenges ahead. Don't worry – by the time you have finished reading this book, you'll be the most prepared personal trainer or online coach in your city.

Fitness businesses seem to be exempt from other business rules. It's the laidback nature of the job and the low barriers to entry. There is a lot they don't teach you on the course, which is why I want this book in the hands of as many who qualify as possible. But let's put business to one side, for now, and talk about the benefits of being a personal trainer. Flexible work hours, tracksuit bottoms for uniform, no gym membership fee, working in a positive environment of change and, most importantly, helping people transform their lives – no exaggeration. It's an incredibly rewarding career. What I find most exciting about it is the journey you go through as a person, not just a coach.

As your career progresses, you will work with all types of people, hearing about and helping solve all types of problems. Because you work with your clients at such an intimate level, you become someone who cares, guides them and offers advice. In doing so, you pick up one of the best skills in life: listening. Not many speak about this, but listening to your clients will transfer seamlessly into your everyday life and will undoubtedly have a positive impact on your future relationships. And once you build those connections and experience the fulfilment this job can offer, you'll realise how much of your potential was being wasted in your previous job, inspiring you even more to give this career everything you've got.

But for every positive the job can offer, it can be met by an equally powerful negative. In fact, the positives I've already mentioned have two sides to them. Flexible working hours sound great at first, but in reality you have to go where the money is. If you are desperate to get your business up and running and a client is ready and willing to pay you, but they only want to train at 6am, you have to get up and do it. It's the sensible thing to do. You end up working unfavourable hours because you haven't done the reps yet.

Changing people's lives might not seem like it can have any downfalls. But as I mentioned before, we work with people on an intimate level. This means your clients rely on you, open up and share personal struggles with you. Once you have 30-plus clients, it can be a lot to take on mentally. On top of your own personal obstacles, challenges and the everyday demands of running a business, this can be overwhelming.

I don't write any of this to put you off. Most reading this will know the feeling. Any great coach wakes up every day with a desire to do the best they can for their clients. Sometimes you need that same soundboard and guidance. I wrote this book to give you that.

Now let's talk about running a fitness business. Your personal training course doesn't cover it. Mine was basically an exam about biology and nutrition, two things that to this day still haven't served me in the real world. Training providers of these qualifications have got better, but they have criteria to follow, and unfortunately, there's no room for a business element. Yet when you finish the course, you need to set up as self-employed, pay your own tax, get your own pension, attract your own customers, and so on. And it shows the minute you get your first job. You start working in a gym, speak to a lovely member who asks for details on personal training with you and you freeze. You have no idea how to take payment, what questions to ask them, what to do with them. Personal training throws you in at the deep end. You may be tempted to connect with other trainers in the gym and ask them what they do. But this isn't the best tactic – you could be the latest in a long line of misguided trainers teaching bad habits and outdated methods.

I want you to know that it's normal to feel that up to now, you've basically been winging it. I did, for three years. I also want you to know that it's normal to think, 'Can I really do this forever?' Well-meaning family members will think of what you do as a 'hobby' and question if it's a real job or not. This is why it's crucial that you surround yourself with people who get it, people who understand the benefits this job has to offer but who equally share experiences on how to overcome its challenges and obstacles. Trust me, every moment of doubt and fear you experience is worth it. This is the best job in the world. All you need is some structure and guidance and you will never look back.

At this point, I'd like to tell you a little more about myself. I own The Glasgow PT company with my fiancée Cheryl. She is the reason I'm in the position I find myself today. When you find someone who supports you every day, your success is inevitable. We recently closed our thriving gym to move the business fully online. We help women look and feel their absolute best. It sounds clichéd but our clients really are wonderful. Cheryl now runs that company, taking it to new heights every single month. That company is one of two six-figure businesses I run. I don't tell you this to brag, but rather to prove what's possible. If I can do it, so can you.

The other business and the reason I'm writing this book is called The Upgraded Coach®. It's designed to help coaches and personal trainers buy a house, travel abroad and love their job. We've helped more than 200 fitness business owners do just that. We've seen clients hit incredible breakthroughs. I'm going to introduce a few of them to you here. But first, let me tell you a couple of other reasons that I wrote this book:

1. The noise. The information around weight loss, nutrition, supplements and exercise is overwhelming. Your job is to cut through the noise, extract what your client needs in their unique situation and formulate a plan to get the desired result.

    Running a fitness business is no different. You will encounter a vast number of opinions and instructions that leave you more confused and stuck than before you heard them. I wrote this book with that in mind. I will cut through the jargon and explain every element of my advice for you.

2. The stats. They don't look great, if I'm honest. It's estimated that twelve months after qualifying,

only 49% of those who qualified are still working as personal trainers.[1] That's more than half of those who spent the money completing the course no longer using it. You only need to be a member of a commercial gym for a few months to see the revolving door of PTs who come in and out. I wrote this book to help more personal trainers stay in the industry long enough to reap the rewards it brings.

The main chapters of this book are made up of the pillars of The Upgraded Coach model: Advanced Belief System, Laser Targeting, Build Authority, Nurture Leads, Irresistible Offer, Epic Education, Solid Systems, Bulletproof Sales Funnel, Slick Sales. These terms may sound strange to you, but don't worry, I will explain every single one of them and why they are important – essentially, looking at these nine pillars will ensure that every element of your fitness business is upgraded.

You will also see frameworks, scripts and diagrams. I've provided all these so that you don't leave with more work. All you'll have to do is apply these up-to-date techniques to your business. There's only one thing I ask of you: to take action. Deal?

Amazing. Ready to get step-by-step guidance? OK, buckle up and get a big notepad ready.

1   L Hughes, 'Personal Trainer Facts & Stats for a Career in Fitness (2021)', Origym (no date), https://origympersonaltrainercourses.co.uk/blog/personal-trainer-facts, accessed 25 November 2022

ONE
The Advanced Belief System

You might be wondering why in the first chapter of a business book, we are chatting about beliefs. Trust me, if we don't get this right, it doesn't matter how many clients sign up with you or how much you love fitness.

Full disclosure, this isn't something I've ever struggled with. It was definitely daunting making the switch from so-called safe employment to being self-employed, but I always believed I'd make it work. I came into the industry at twenty-five years old. I had experienced life a bit and the customer service skills I had gained were fully transferable into coaching. Newly qualified personal trainers seem to be getting younger and younger and I absolutely love how well they do at twenty, twenty-one. I certainly wasn't ready to be an adult at that age.

The Advanced Belief System is multi-layered. It's about guarding your inputs to avoid your journey being derailed. It's being connected to a community of fellow trainers and trusted advisors, and it's realising that you *can* make this job as successful as people say. You *can* prove people wrong who dismissed this as a career. By working on your belief system, you create a perfect environment for personal and business growth.

The inevitable doubt, worry and second-guessing can all be managed when we get this right. No one is immune to these thoughts and feelings – it's how we navigate them that can either make us a successful coach or make us become part of the 51% who leave the profession too soon.

Communication is key

'Isn't this just a hobby? How are you going to make a living from that?'

You may have had this conversation already with your parents or loved ones. They see you going to the gym, then you tell them that actually, you love fitness and you want to pursue a career as a personal trainer. Initially, they may be happy for you. But eventually, it comes to a crossroads. Your parents are being asked, 'Aw, what's your son/daughter doing now?' They reply with 'Personal training', followed by some added reasoning to make it sound better than it is. The truth is, parents don't know a lot about it. They think it's adult PE. They don't understand that in today's world, a personal trainer has the potential to become part of the top 5% of earners in the UK.

So how do we combat this and get our parents and loved ones on board? Communication. Sit down with them and explain how passionate you are about this. Explain that you have spoken to more experienced trainers and you can see the possibilities. They don't have to understand the ins and outs of your business, but they have to be clear that you are serious about this and that you'd love for them to support you. I've seen situations where coaches have gone from making £3k to £4k per month coaching to leaving the industry for a 'safe' job on their parents' instruction, earning *less*. But because it's 'guaranteed' pay, they've taken it. Again, parents mean well, but they don't understand how it works.

With all that said, it's equally important that you play your part. Your parents, loved ones and peers won't take it seriously if you don't. If you want to prove them wrong, you need to be fully invested in your clients, in improving your service and prioritising self-development.

The three challenges you will face

There isn't a personal trainer on the planet exempt from facing these challenges at some point in their career – sometimes they pay you a visit in a single week. It's best you are prepared so that you can deal with them when they come along.

Challenge 1: Shiny objects

Nothing will derail you from building up momentum and consistency in your fitness business quite like chasing some shiny new trend. Don't get me wrong, it's important to be open to trying new things, but it's about identifying your need for whatever that is.

Take your clients for example – you send them a tailored plan, and they are two weeks in and enjoying the process. But Sarah down the road is two weeks into her latest diet trend that consists of licking a rare plant found in the rainforest, which happens to have been bottled and is £9.99 in every shop. Sarah drops 8 lbs in one week. She tells your client this and it makes your client feel disheartened, considering personal training is a lot more expensive than £9.99 and the results much less instant. Of course, we know that poor Sarah has simply been sucked into the latest diet trend and unfortunately for her, she's probably going to put all the weight back on and/or pass out from the lack of food. But your client has just been distracted from your tailored plan by a shiny new object.

The same can be said for your business. You speak to other trainers in your gym, follow them on social media and they all seem to be doing so well. Perhaps some of them were even on the same course as you. The world likes to make you think there are secrets to their success – secret morning routines, secret hacks, secret business tactics. The truth is, there aren't any. I want you to get good at putting on the blinkers. Block out what others are doing and stay on your own track.

It's easy to get distracted in this social network-obsessed world. Everything is right in your face and if you don't filter out the noise, you can become a victim of trying out the latest fancy graphics, viral videos and social media bandwagons. If you continue to start new projects and chase new shiny objects, you'll prevent yourself from finishing what else you are doing, leaving you frustrated at the lack of progress.

Challenge 2: Guesswork

A lot of running a business is learning on the job. As we've mentioned, you qualify with very few tools at your disposal, so you can try things, see what works and what doesn't – and remember, what works for one trainer doesn't necessarily work for another. But learning on the job can take a long time, especially if you don't have a support network around you. There are fundamentals that you can have in place to build a solid business and I will be sharing all of them with you.

This book will remove years of guesswork for you. I spent three years winging it and it almost led to me quitting. It's strange for me to think back to that point, because the right information and help was out there all along. I just couldn't see it for all the noise.

I urge you to make a promise to yourself that whatever you invest time and money in, make sure to remove the guesswork. Make sure it's in learning tried-and-tested systems. The sooner you build in structure to your business, the sooner your confidence grows and momentum increases, creating a snowball effect.

Challenge 3: Imposter syndrome

Imposter syndrome can be loosely defined as doubting your abilities and feeling like a fraud. This will hit you the minute you take your first ever PT session. It's a bit like passing your driving test and finally taking the car out on your own. After qualifying, you realise that now you are in the big bad world and you have to look after yourself.

Imposter syndrome has become a bit of a buzzword recently, and not just in fitness circles. In most cases, it's a label for the lack of confidence you experience when entering uncharted territory. There are many reasons why trainers can feel low in confidence – comparison to other people's businesses, bodies and lives, or pressure from society or family to live up to their expectations.

So how do we deal with imposter syndrome? I'm going to give you the best way, but first, here's an extra bonus way. Get help. When you have someone more experienced than you to use as a soundboard, your ideas and decisions are backed up. You carry them out with the conviction that what you are doing will work, based on your mentor's sage advice. You can't focus on being an imposter when you are busy delivering.

And now let's look at the best way to never feel like a fraud again.

Play to your strengths

I'm not the wishy-washy manifestation-of-your-goals-out-to-the-universe kind of guy. I believe that taking action is the cure for struggles with your mindset. This part of the book isn't about getting you to stand up, roar and tell the world how amazing you are. It's about identifying your strengths as a person and trainer.

When we know what our strengths are, we harness them and use them to face challenges and make tough decisions. Again, imposter syndrome doesn't stand a chance if you're busy doing what you're great at. On the flip side, identifying your strengths will also show you your areas that need more work, so that you can get better at them and make yourself a better business owner.

For me, coaching and chatting to members on the gym floor came naturally. It was the organisation of the backend business that I struggled with (tracking income, clients' sessions, tax dates, etc). So I hired an accountant and paid for software to remove the headache. Improving on the things you aren't as good at alongside making the most of your strengths will make you an incredibly well-rounded coach who clients will pay a lot of money to work with.

TASK: How to identify your strengths

1. **Listen to feedback.** If you've got clients, review your most recent testimonials. What is the common theme? Maybe they are saying how supportive you are, how much you care or how relatable you are.

2. **Consider your passions.** Many personal trainers overlook life skills and how they can fit them into their business. For example, if you are creative and artistic, this can be transferred to creating client documents, developing marketing campaigns, or making engaging training plans. If you are confident, outspoken and charismatic, you could create engaging video content, make client education resources and deliver live coaching calls. Put the skills you are passionate about to use, because they're your superpower.

3. **Pay attention to when you are most productive.** Throughout your day-to-day activities, make a note of how long different tasks take and how productive you are. If it feels like time is passing

---

quickly and you accomplish a lot in a short period, you are likely using some of your biggest strengths. Make a list of when you feel the most focused and consider what characteristics motivate you during those times. If you notice that time drags on during certain tasks, see if you can identify what makes you feel less motivated so that you can either avoid those situations or try to develop those skills.

4. **Ask.** A simple one: ask friends, family and clients what your biggest strengths are. Don't be hard on yourself, either. If someone tells you a specific strength, don't argue with them – add it to the list.

Now you have an idea of your strengths, work to make the most of them.

Tell your story

I mentioned the word 'superpower' in relation to your strengths, but it also applies to your story. One of the few tools you have at your disposal when you qualify is telling your story. It's an essential part of building trust with your audience and it's a great way for you to introduce yourself.

TV shows like *Big Brother*, *Love Island* and *Gogglebox* all surged in popularity because people love watching people. We are nosey. This is important to note, because by telling your story you're giving people what they want. Speak about your past exercise experience, why you became a personal trainer and what your current goals are, and your followers will find this inspiring. It gives them an insight into your personality and, ideally, leads to them wanting to work with you. It also sets you on a healthy path of putting yourself out there. Otherwise, you'll find yourself trying to fit the mould and end up coming across as generic.

What's great about telling your story is you don't have to overthink it. It's real life. Let's make sure you continue to show your human side, document your personal life, goals and hobbies. Remember, people buy from people. If you only share serious fitness content and leave your personality out of your posts, your audience will feel disconnected from you.

Guard your inputs

Another way that you can be sidetracked from your vision is by listening to the opinions of others. Let's take an example of a client – we'll call him Bob. Bob is desperate to lose fat and build muscle. He's failed to do so on all three previous attempts. This time, he's adamant it will work. He hires two personal trainers thinking this will double his chances of success. He sees PT#1 on Mondays and PT#2 on Wednesdays. Neither PT advises this but Bob is adamant. He gets two nutrition plans and two training plans.

What are Bob's chances of success? Is he better off with one or two PTs? It's clearly one, and the reason is that more doesn't mean better. Bob threw the kitchen sink at his fitness regime because he didn't want to fail again. But the more opinions, voices and people you let in, the more confused you will be. The same applies to business. It doesn't mean you should listen to the same person for the remainder of your career, but just be wary of any mixed messages coming your way.

A great quote is, 'Never take advice from someone you wouldn't trade places with.' You can still listen to your gran's solid life advice, but pay attention to the context the advice is coming from. If a fellow PT is offering you advice but they've been in the same gym for the last five years and still work shifts, maybe take their advice with a pinch of salt. If the advice is coming from a family member who's never run a business, maybe take it with a pinch of salt.

When trainers sign up to The Upgraded Coach, I ask the question, 'Are you guarding your inputs?' From the 200-plus people who have signed up, I can count on one hand how many have said, 'Yes.' Most don't realise just how important it is.

Take social media for example. Part of growing your business is putting yourself out there, whether by talking on camera, uploading videos of your training, or creating an informative post. All will have great benefits to your followers, but equally, people will have something negative to say. You will have people following you who don't want to see you do well. When I first started speaking on camera, I had people message me saying that I was putting an accent on. This is them trying to have 'banter', but in reality, they are showing their true colours. If I wasn't thick-skinned, comments like that might have put me off talking to the camera again, resulting in me not putting myself out there, not improving my confidence and not offering value to my audience. Can you see how not guarding your inputs can actually have an impact on your business?

It's important we get used to ignoring comments that don't serve us. Feedback and constructive criticism are useful, as long as they come from a valid source you respect. An old school pal making comments about you and your business is not a respectful source. Ignore.

Invest time in your business

When you start to fill your coaching diary, you'll end up working anywhere from thirty to forty sessions per week of personal training. This is what is classed as working 'in' the business. It's your bread and butter. But to be a great coach and business owner, you have to be doing more.

Your six-week qualification may have felt long, but in the grand scheme of things, it was nothing. To become a better coach, you must set aside time to learn, read and research. One thing that took a while to click in my head was that coaching on the gym floor every day and checking in with clients on weekends wasn't growing the business. Those are the deliverables that clients pay for. You have to do more in order to grow.

This becomes trickier the more in demand you become, and while rolling up your sleeves and getting the work done is great, there will come a time when you either burn out or you max out your income. The skills that help you keep busy won't help you earn more, or even earn the same for less work. But this isn't just about business or growth. It's a warning that you have to be protective of your energy and prioritise yourself. Coaching is a selfless job and if you're not careful, you can end up pouring from an empty cup.

Finding a work–life balance with a job you love is tough. Business matters, personal matters, downtime, your own training, fun and family all have to be considered when planning out your days and weeks. I know how hard this can be, so I've created a document that has helped skyrocket our coaches' day-to-day energy management and productivity. Grab your free download from my website and complete it to start a new week. It only takes five minutes.[2]

Invest money in your business

Most businesses start off by immediately investing: restaurants hire staff and buy food, tradesmen buy tools and transport. Most trainers qualify and,

---

2   https://chris-bradley.co.uk/resources

because they've just paid for their qualification, they keep their money in their wallet.

Thankfully, you've got this book. But it can't stop there. Remember the skill sets you might be lacking that we spoke about earlier? They're a good place to start investing money in. Courses, education and support are your best bet. They should help you reduce the guesswork, keep you focused on your mission, keep you accountable and improve your confidence to deliver.

Not every investment has a guaranteed return. But neither does a client's investment in you. A client pays for your expertise to remove their own guess-work and cut through the noise, to give them a plan, to hold them to a higher standard than they've been holding themselves to and to get them a result. It's verging on hypocritical if you aren't doing the same when it comes to your business.

Look, this is me speaking to my past self as well. It was three years before I invested back into my business. Buying Nike trainers, chalk and a belt doesn't count. But as you will find out, it was almost my downfall.

Be prepared to spend. Mentorships, self-development and marketing are all great places to invest in first. If you're looking for another book recommendation to get you started, check out *Mindset* by Carol Dweck.[3]

---

3   CS Dweck, *Mindset: How you can fulfil your potential* (Robinson, 2012)

CASE STUDY - CHLOE

Let me introduce you to one of our longest serving clients, Chloe. When she signed up, she was working another job and had just qualified. Her biggest concern was leaving the stable income of her job for what seemed to be the 'unpredictable' income of training. She powered through and started building and marketing her service. But there was only so much she could do because the night shifts in her other job left her exhausted. With not enough hours in the day, she was feeling frustrated.

On top of this, she couldn't fully commit. Her clients knew she had another job, and while that's not a bad thing, clients don't want to be part of someone's part-time hobby, especially with something as serious as their health and fitness.

At this point, Chloe's belief system was understandably fragile. There were days she was so exhausted she questioned if it was all worth it. She continued to invest time and money into the process and that's when everything started to change.

We set out a three-stage plan. First, we had to build a professional service – one that wowed a client when they came on board and that Chloe could be proud of. Then we set targets to hit that would enable Chloc to leave her other job. This was the hardest part, because time was precious, so it was vital we only focused on the things that could get her there. We needed to know how many clients she needed and at what price point to replace her other wage. Importantly, we had to agree on a timescale and be accountable to it. Otherwise, fatigue and burnout would creep in.

Once the clients started coming in, Chloe's confidence skyrocketed. With only ten clients, she could replace her previous job's salary.

Now Chloe is a full-time PT and online coach. She's created a community of like-minded women who get together frequently to be educated, inspired and have fun. Her client–result portfolio is growing in line with her reputation in her gym and city.

She is also a great contributor to The Upgraded Coach community. Chloe is equal parts generous and ambitious – my favourite type of coach.

Summary

- Improving your mindset is crucial to the success of your fitness business. Communicate firmly with those who see it as a hobby and take your business seriously. Have people around you who get it.

- Be aware of the three biggest challenges you will face throughout your career. These come and go, so don't be disheartened that you can't master them: shiny objects, guesswork and imposter syndrome.

- Dial in on your unique superpowers. There will be times you compare yourself to others, but remember that context is a wonderful thing and more often than not, we don't know the full story. Put on your blinkers and head for your own finish line.

- Identify your strengths, then play to those strengths and home in on the areas you are great at. Watch your confidence soar. Whatever your strengths are, it might be useful to stick your list to your computer screen to constantly be reminded.

- Go ahead and tell your own unique story – personal as well as professional. This is the easiest way to build a connection with your followers. Some people find it intimidating to reach out to a personal trainer. Break down that barrier by showing your human side and being relatable.

- Guard your inputs to reduce the noise and likelihood of distraction and stop irrelevant outside influences from getting in your head. Be open-minded but question the sources of any advice coming your way. Aim to have a group of inspiring peers to bounce ideas off.

- Make sure you have a good balance of working *on* and *in* the business. Invest time to improve your own knowledge and, as a result, the service you give to your clients. Put money back into the business. If you want clients who are prepared to invest to learn and get a result, you have to be willing to do the same.

TWO
Laser Targeting

Laser targeting shapes your whole marketing strategy. It's about identifying who you are targeting to become paying clients – who do you want to work with? It is essential to know that you can't help everyone. If you try to, you end up with mixed and diluted messaging.

What makes our approach laser-focused is that there are several steps to it. We don't just make it gender-specific. We analyse our ideal client's psychographics – their activities, interests, opinions, fears, frustrations, wants, aspirations, etc. If you understand these, you understand the person in front of you. You know what they need, and you can tell them you have the solution.

When you create content for social media or email, you must know who you are speaking to. As you type, think, 'Who is this for? How do I want them to feel reading it? What do I want them to do?' Once you know that, writing the content becomes effortless. In this chapter, we'll create your audience with a ton of clarity to make your message laser targeted.

This chapter isn't the longest in the book, but it's the most important, so please take action on the short tasks provided. You will reap the benefits of having complete clarity about who you help and what you help them with. You will end up with a service full of people you love helping – now that is job fulfilment.

Target the message to your clients

If you imagine a huge fishing net, the bigger the net, the bigger the holes. They are designed to cover as big an area as possible. What happens, though, is the net catches 'bycatch'. This is when they catch fish they don't want to, didn't intend to or are not allowed to catch.

Your fitness business is the same. When you post generic content, you end up attracting people you don't want, people you can't help or people who aren't a good fit for your service. If you're struggling to get the clients you're looking for, then the answer lies in adjusting your messaging.

Remember earlier I said, 'People buy from people'?
They also buy through relatability. If your prospects
can see that you are just a trainer who likes socialising
at the weekends, enjoys training and has kids, people
in a similar position will notice. They will want to know
how to stay in shape while enjoying themselves at
weekends. They will want to know how to eat healthy
while being a busy parent. Now can you once again see
how important it is for you to tell your story?

Here's an example of how being specific in your messaging can attract the right audience. Take a look at
these headings:

- 'Do I have to eat breakfast in the morning?'
  (generic post)

- 'Healthy grab-n-go recipes for busy parents'
  (specific post)

In the second heading, I've taken the target market –
busy parents – and addressed a common struggle they
experience. They usually have such a frantic morning getting kids ready for school that they don't have
time to sit down themselves and have breakfast. This
could impact their nutrition. Imagine after the school
run when hunger sets in, the temptation to grab a hot
greasy roll could be too much. Instead, we can offer a
solution for that exact scenario.

You can see how that post has the power to hit home
and show the reader that you know their struggles.

That builds a ton of trust and moves them closer to enquiring about your service.

TASK: Change your generic content to specific

Go over your last ten pieces of content. Are they addressing a specific target market, or are they generic?

Redo the generic ones. You don't have to make new content, just add a target market and give an example of their situation. It's likely that these posts won't get as many likes because they are specific. But you will get more people bought into you – the essential metric in your business marketing.

Narrow your niche

How do we stop marketing to everyone and saying the same as every other personal trainer? We choose our niche. This is our target market, or 'avatar', as a professional marketer might use to identify a specific person as an example, such as 'busy mums over forty who are fed up yo-yo dieting'. Your avatar could be your existing client, Mary. You know Mary's specific challenges, so with that knowledge, you could go out and market effectively to find more clients like Mary.

Choosing our niche means we go from big net, large holes, to smaller net, smaller holes. Will this catch less 'fish'? Absolutely. But it's important to understand that less is more when growing your coaching business. As

I said, you can't help everyone, nor do you want to. You work with people on such an intimate level that it can feel forced, awkward and miserable if they're not a good match for you.

There can be an argument made against choosing a niche. For those who are just starting, you need clients, and training different types of people can help you decide sooner who you want to help specifically later on. Unfortunately for most trainers, they don't stop. Then three big problems occur:

1. They continue to market to everyone, ending up with four or five different types of clients in the programme. This stops them from creating a comprehensive service and results in a revolving door of clients in and out.

2. They get frustrated with low client adherence. But it's not the clients' fault, it's the service that isn't a fit for them.

3. They don't know what to post. Because they are exposed to all these different problems from a mixed bag of clients, their content changes daily. As this content gets less and less traction, their confidence takes a hit.

Dial in on your niche but be open to it changing – ie, 'Date your niche, don't marry it.' I think this is crucial because as you grow as a person and coach, you mature and develop new skills. You might have once helped young students lose weight on a budget. But now you're twenty-six and want to help busy professionals. By dating your niche, you give yourself time to see what content works, if you work well with those people, and if you can get them a result. Then as you adapt and change, your client base can too.

Speak your clients' language

I promised that I would keep this book jargon-free. I'd love for you to do the same with your marketing and messaging. There will be buzzwords that you learned in your course that you want to use. Sorry to break it to you, but your clients don't care about correct terminology and don't need to know. Using words and phrases that confuse and alienate your audience is the opposite of being relatable. It creates a divide and a disconnect. The unique situation where this doesn't apply is if you end up coaching professional athletes, but it's most likely you won't. So let's speak the language of your niche.

This simple model shows the different categories we fall under when writing content. That category or role affects the agenda of your content.

Take a look at the circle below. Follow the arc from each role and you get to the agenda. Let's look at these in turn:

Coach > Performance. Think like a coach, and you focus on performance. You break down the intricacies of an exercise and offer up coaching cues. You suggest improvements that can be made to lift more or perform better.

Marketer > Persuasion. Think like a marketer, and you talk about what your product or service can do. You create excitement around its features and benefits. You add a sense of urgency and scarcity and a call to action. The aim is to persuade the reader to take action and buy your stuff.

Prospect > Problem. Think like a prospect, and you automatically think of your current audience's frustrations. The reader thinks you are reading their mind or have a spy camera in their house because it's exactly how they feel. Can you see how nicely this fits into targeting your niche?

It's important to note that not every piece of content you produce has to be about frustrations. But it should make up the bulk of your messaging. Relatability is king.

Become your prospect

So how do we think about our prospects? We have to become them. This isn't the part where we play dress-up and put our standard-grade drama skills to use, but where we answer the following questions:

1. What's your target market's biggest desire? What do they want? (Eg, to get in shape.)

2. Why do they want that? Remember, it's not just what would happen, but what would that give them. (Eg, they want to get in shape so that they feel more attractive, more confident in life resulting in a promotion, finding love, etc)

3. What's their biggest problem or frustration? What's the number-one obstacle holding them back? (Eg, lack of time.)

4. How is that impacting them emotionally? You want to get the specific emotions here and the situation. (Eg, they feel low and are time-poor, so they turn to comfort/convenience food, which makes them feel worse and creates a vicious cycle.)

A downloadable table is available on my website for you to fill out these questions with your target clients in mind.[4] Take your time with this and if you're stuck, think of a current client who fits this avatar. What do they struggle with? What's their big goal?

Once you have filled out this table, keep the completed version on your desk. The answers will inspire everything you create for your service. The clarity it gives you when explaining who you help and what you help them with is invaluable.

TASK: Get inside your prospect's head

Imagine your prospect's mind consumed with the desire to experience the outcome you described. Picture them worrying over their biggest problem and how it's holding them back. With that scene so precise in your mind, pretend you are them and finish this sentence: 'If I could just...'

This task will not only provide you with a lot of ideas for future content you can write, but it will allow you to develop empathy for your prospects and deepen your connection with them, so that you can serve them better.

---

4   https://chris-bradley.co.uk/resources

CASE STUDY – HOLLI

Holli is a gym owner and online coach in Glasgow. Like 95% of coaches, she had a one-size-fits-all service. There was a wide variety of clients in her gym, so it made sense to create a variety of resources. The problems started to appear when client adherence dropped significantly. Clients weren't checking in with her. They were cancelling sessions and not adhering to their nutrition or training plans. This caused Holli a lot of stress as she did everything she could to provide them with the tools they needed.

It became clear that the variety of clients meant Holli was chasing her tail trying to cater to a whole host of different problems. Some clients felt alienated. Some felt seen and heard. Like most coaches, we blame ourselves and think we aren't doing enough.

When we create content for clients that doesn't hit home, we question our skill set. This translates to our marketing, because if we're creating content for clients and it doesn't work, surely it's not going to appeal to a bunch of strangers? When Holli went to write a piece of content, it felt like a chore and she was unsure who it was even for.

It was time to take action. The first thing we did was choose Holli a niche. Once we decided, it was time for her to become her prospects. She started putting a crystal-clear message out there and her confidence grew. She filled her gym with clients who shared similar struggles and frustrations. This meant she could create resources and build a service to solve those struggles. Adherence increased, client engagement in the group soared and results flooded in.

At the time of writing this, Holli has just hired another coach to work with her in her gym. For context, Holli has only been in the industry a year and a half and has already gone from being a small studio owner to upsizing to a more extensive and thriving facility. She has a gym with one of the best community aspects I've seen, full of women lifting heavy and building a strong culture – incredible work from a coach who invested time and money into her business the minute she left her qualification. I'm so proud.

Summary

- If you aren't getting clients as frequently as you'd like, your messaging could be falling short. Auditing your content and changing generic posts to specific posts will increase their appeal to your target audience.

- Marketing to everyone can get you traction and help you reach a bigger audience, but a more extensive reach can result in a diluted and less impactful message, so try not to get drawn into sounding like every other coach.

- Complete the quick task of narrowing your niche. Don't overthink it, and remember to 'date the niche'. Think of having twenty-five A-grade clients who you love helping. What would that do for your business, your enjoyment and fulfilment?

- Speak your prospects' language to build a connection and avoid alienating them. Your prospects don't care about the science behind exercise and nutrition. They just want to be assured you know their problems and how to fix them.

- Become your prospect. You will be able to fully understand their struggles, articulate them and build a service that solves them. You will be rewarded with much higher engagement, more qualified leads and consistent enquiries.

- Be relatable and share your personal story. Your prospects will notice and start to see that you get it. Transparency and honesty will fill your diary quicker than any marketing hack.

THREE

Build Authority

Once you qualify, you will start to overthink the tactical parts of your coaching. You'll wonder, 'How many calories should I put Tracy on?' or, 'What kind of training split will I give to Paul?' It's understandable that you would. But for the most part, it doesn't matter. It's not why they came to you.

For the first few years, your best bet is to spend more time thinking about a massively overlooked element – authority. Your authority can be the difference between you and the other personal trainers in your gym. It's what makes you stand out. Your authority in your gym, your city, with your clients and with your peers.

In this chapter, we are going to talk about what authority is, why it's so important and the three key elements to establishing your authority asap. Let's dive in.

What is authority?

First let's start with what it's *not*. It's not you becoming an old-school fitness instructor wearing army trousers and running a bootcamp in the rain. It's not you being strict or barking orders at your clients. So what is it? It's building up respect. It's conducting yourself in a way that is professional and approachable. It's showing up and being a role model.

If you've followed me for a while, you'll know that one of my most repeated messages is this: 'Watch what others do, then avoid it.' If your fellow coaches sit around the staff room on their phones, don't do it. If they show up just on time for clients or classes, don't do it. It's funny that *not* doing something can make you stand out. It requires no effort other than to resist the temptation to do the same as everyone else. But when you do this, you will stand out in your gym and your authority will go up.

Authority affects people's perception of you, particularly your prospects'. When they read your content or engage with you in the gym, they can sense your authority. They believe that you are the person they should ask for help.

Three client benefits of having authority

Benefit 1: Client adherence

When new clients come on board, they are apprehensive. They've just spent their hard-earned money to get help for something they don't particularly enjoy, to sacrifice foods they love and to do things that make them feel uncomfortable. It's crucial we get them to buy in to the process early on. It's our job to make them realise that the money they've spent on their fitness is worth it, that they actually don't have to sacrifice foods they love and they can feel comfortable with this new activity.

The quickest and most effective way to get their buy in is to show them what's possible. When they join, if they are surrounded by like-minded individuals who are as busy as them, of similar age, and have similar likes and dislikes, then they immediately realise that what they want is possible. When the outcome is more believable, client adherence improves.

Some coaches beat themselves up when clients aren't adhering to their plans. They question their worth and feel like a fraud. They also question the approach they've given the client to get the result. As I mentioned earlier, it's not about the plans. It's about the relationship between coach and client. Sure, we could list a ton of reasons why they aren't sticking to things, but one of the biggest factors is the level of your authority.

45

Without authority, your clients won't be able to connect the dots and truly make use of what you're offering. But if they sign up and are met with professional videos of you explaining your service and breaking down their next steps, they will be fully engaged as a new client and know that they are part of something serious. With more authority, you will have fewer cancellations, fewer no-shows and fewer late-comers. Clients will value your time and won't want to waste it.

Benefit 2: Client retention

When clients get results, they tend to stay and pay. As long as you're keeping things exciting in your programme, they won't leave, especially not to another coach. If you become the go-to guy or girl in your gym or local area, the authority box is ticked. Why would your clients go elsewhere? You're as good as it gets.

There isn't a more powerful tool in business than retaining clients. It's what stops you from having to go looking for more. It's what builds a solid, predictable business and gives you complete confidence that you're doing a great job.

Benefit 3: Client acquisition

You're getting great results, clients are staying and you're the go-to coach in your gym. How does that look for attracting new clients? Well, it looks pretty good.

Your happy clients will refer their friends, family and co-workers to you. They are walking, talking adverts and can't sing your praises highly enough. They talk about you in the staff canteen. If you get lucky, you could end up training a full office. Your business will run on referrals, reducing your need to market as much.

People will approach you in the gym to ask about your services because they've seen you so much on the gym floor coaching clients. They will wait behind at the end of your classes to engage and ask questions.

All of this sounds idealistic. But it's true. It really is the impact that established authority can have on your business. Now let's look at how you can achieve that.

Top tips for establishing your authority

Tip 1: Fill your classes

The first week into my first personal training job, I got thrown in at the deep end. Another coach missed their train and suddenly, a lunchtime spin class with thirty people had no instructor. I hadn't been trained on how to take one yet. But, like everything in your personal training career, you learn by doing. With no uniform and no playlist, I entered the spin studio for the first time. For the more experienced coaches reading this, you'll know that a great playlist with upbeat tracks timed perfectly to hill climbs and sprints makes a great spin class.

It's also worth noting that I preferred lifting weights. My football days were long gone so my cardio game wasn't the best. Not only that, but I had never used a spin bike in my life. But I was eager to impress my new manager and step up when they needed me. I'll never forget those thirty faces staring back at me awaiting instructions. Four or five of the loyal attendees were probably thinking, 'Eh, who are you?!' I quickly introduced myself and went on with the class. It was messy but my optimism and fresh take on it helped them get a proper sweat on. Me? I was hooked.

I spent the next three years fully invested in making my classes better by the week. I thrived in a busy class environment and when I had fewer than twenty people in one, it genuinely put me in a mood. I would go searching the gym floor five minutes before to get people involved and fill the class up. I became known for my classes and this helped fill my coaching diary. The more people I had at my classes, the more people knew me, and I'd sign up clients from those people. The best part was, I never tried to push PT. Thinking back, this wasn't a tactic – I was just caught up in delivering value.

Further down the line, I'd look around my class and 70% of the attendees were clients. They had all become clients off the back of coming to my classes, which were the most in-demand on the timetable. I owe a lot to those classes. My confidence skyrocketed.

Situations in gyms are different now. You're unlikely to have thirty people in a gym-based class. But you don't need that many; ten is enough. Make sure your classes are valuable, engaging and exciting. Take pride in them and don't just expect people to book in. Walk the gym floor and invite people. Share your slots on your social media. Think of classes as an audition. You have a few prospects in front of you who are sussing you out to see if they will pay you to coach them.

Do not approach your classes with the mindset that the session is free and people don't want your help. Other coaches in your gym might show up just on time – or worse, late – then do the same routines every week and generally make it obvious they don't want to be there. Remember, if you avoid doing that, you'll stand out.

Tip 2: Develop your business outreach

Business outreach is one of the most underused tools for building authority. Usually this is because coaches think, 'I could never do that,' and they don't. Which makes it your secret weapon. Business outreach is essentially networking with local businesses and workplaces in your city, including but not limited to businesses near the gym you work in. Examples include delivering a talk to those companies' staff or putting on a lunchtime fitness class for the office.

Most companies have an obligation to ensure they are promoting a healthy working environment for their colleagues. Some even set aside a 'wellness budget' to pay a gym or personal trainer to fulfil this need. They take it pretty seriously and include it as one of their employment benefits. We can make the most of that by networking with them to give them an 'exclusive offer' for their company.

I was fortunate enough that my client at the time arranged my very first networking event. It wasn't huge – about sixteen people in a room. It was one hour long and my topic was, 'Making healthy choices on your lunch break'. I did it with one of my best mates, Connor. We were pretty nervous going into it, but one thing that surprised us was just how different it was from taking a class in the gym. You realise that's your stomping ground. You can lead thirty people, motivate them and run the class like a pro. But remove yourself from that environment and suddenly you are nervous and out of your comfort zone. It's like playing a football match away from home.

It's time to do what most of the coaches in your gym aren't willing to: arrange a talk at a local business. The best place to start is with your current clients and their workplaces. They know the right people to ask, they can talk you up and arrange most of it for you.

Set a date, get an understanding of their struggles, create a topic that solves those problems and deliver it. You will immediately be noticed as an authority in your field. Remember to document your talk for promotional content.

Here's a script to send a client and get the ball rolling:

Hey [NAME], just like you, I have BIG goals for [YEAR]. One of them is to impact as many people as possible in [YOUR CITY].

I'd love your help! I'm looking for you to nominate your workplace for a live seminar. This would involve me coming in, for free, to speak to your colleagues about health and fitness. I can deliver this talk on a particular subject to ensure it's valuable for them.

I know there are a lot of companies out there who are prioritising the wellness of their colleagues. Just wondering if you could connect me with the person who I need to speak to and then we can get a date locked in!

Thank you!

Tip 3: Optimise your social media

We could spend this section looking at what's working great right now for growing your business on social media. But the truth is this rapidly changes month to month, so to avoid sharing what might end up being outdated tactics, let me share with you the fundamentals to put in place. I won't be sharing how to go viral or how to get more likes. Sorry, but those vanity metrics wear off and I'm all about long-term business strategies. As you read through this section, I want you to think about your social media pages and how they measure up against the advice below.

Where do we start? **First glance.** In today's world, we only have people's attention for seconds. The first glance a prospect takes at your business page is important. Your **bio** is the piece where you explain exactly who you are, who you help and what you help them with. Make this short, snappy and clear, though it can be longer if on a website (more on that in Chapter 8).

Then we have the **most recent images**. When we are creating content, we go through phases of posting certain styles. It could be a more informative style, more personal images, or more videos. It's not a bad thing, but just for a second, take a look at your most recent posts through the eyes of a prospect. Is there variation? Clients, your programme, social proof and value should all be easy to see. Sometimes we go all in on one of those. By assessing your pictures now and again and taking action accordingly, you can keep the variety up and give a well-rounded picture of your business.

Lastly, look at your **display picture**. Certain platforms allow you to have a profile picture. I'm no expert but

I do know that a quality professional headshot would be a good idea. If you have more space to play with, an image of you training clients or at a client community event would be even better. Avoid dark, unprofessional shots, ie, with your top off.

Making **contact** with you should be easy on your business page. (You have no idea how many coaches overlook this.) A clear **CTA (call to action)** should be visible. 'Click the link below' is usually enough.

That takes us on to our next part, the **link**. This is usually a clickable link displayed on your page that takes your prospects to an enquiry form. They will then input their details, register their interest and maybe even book a call. If the link isn't there, you are relying on the prospect messaging you privately and coming up with what to say. Believe it or not, they'd much rather fill in a form and share a bit about their journey. Later on, we will help you build that enquiry form, so stay tuned.

Having a clear CTA and a link is great. But it has to be simple. **Simplicity** is crucial when it comes to your prospects getting in touch. If the link takes an age to load, or it makes them log in to complete a form, you will leave money on the table.

Think of your business page as a shop window. If you walked past a shop and the shutters were down, would you still be interested? Nope. You'd walk straight past it without a second look. It's the same for your page. A clear 'come on in' approach will get clients in the door.

It goes without saying that if you want to grow your business and attract more clients on social media, your **content** has to hit the mark. **Branding** is one way to do that. For those of you unsure what branding is, it's the *why* you do the things you do – why you are a coach and why people should work with you. It builds loyalty and trust with people. It's also crucial for finding more people who share the same ethics, values and beliefs as you. After all, you'll get on really well with them. People become drawn to what you have to offer. They will see your personality, your programmes that are changing people's lives and the community you are building.

Please note – do not be the best-kept secret with this. Looking after clients is priority number one, but a close second is showcasing your service. Show the world your brand. Show them how great you are. Don't be cheap with this. It's no longer acceptable to have a dumbbell or kettlebell as your business logo. Transformations, clothing, resources and value posts should contain your new shiny branding, and your business ethics and values should be apparent in your content. All of this will have a positive impact on your marketing – and your product is the marketing, so shout from the rooftop and put it out there.

Marketing is an Achilles heel for some coaches. By their own admission, they hate marketing their services. They didn't know it was in the job description when they qualified. If this is you, it's OK, because help is at hand. If branding is the *why*, then marketing is the *how*. How will you get clients from where they are now to where they want to be? What tools will you use to get a response from your audience? How will you get more people engaging with your content? How can you generate more leads?

Marketing can be a powerful thing, especially in today's noisy world. Nailing your marketing can be the thing that makes you stand out. Your marketing strategy should be visible on your social media pages, eg, in one-time offers, 'love it or leave it' trials, new product launches, etc.

The most important thing to show on your social media channels is a showcase of your **results**. This is not necessarily before and after images, but whatever is the 'wow' factor that your niche market wants. That is what will get you traction and spark interest in your services. You could use images, testimonials, milestones in your clients' lives and journey with you. Whatever the thing is that stops your target client from scrolling and gets them thinking, 'I need that!'

When all is said and done, your role is about helping a person achieve exactly what they set out to do. Nothing will convince a prospect to sign up with you more than them seeing, reading or listening to one of your clients who was in a very similar position to them before signing up with you and has now transformed their life.

Let me ask you this: how would you rate your current authority in your gym or city? How well-known are you for doing what you do? Answer this and you'll have clarity on what to do next.

CASE STUDY – BRENDON

Allow me to introduce you to another fantastic Upgraded Coach – Brendon. Before joining us, he blended in with other coaches in his gym despite knowing he could offer so much more. After the recent pandemic, he felt lost, uninspired and underconfident and was afraid of being average.

Outside his gym, he was relatively unknown. This made attracting new clients very difficult. He wasn't building additional elements to his service and, as a result, was only getting client results if they worked with him in a one-to-one capacity.

Before we created new systems and products, it was clear we had to get Brendon's mojo back. He knew a lot of what had to be done, but without accountability, a support network and a plan, he was falling short.

We clarified Brendon's values and what he wanted his business to become. Nothing is more refreshing than working on your business when it's built on *your* true beliefs and no one else's.

Next it was time to add services to his business. Working long hours one-to-one was beginning to get tiring, and to break through income caps and avoid total burnout, we had to leverage his time. We added small group training and online coaching programmes. This allowed him to taper off one-to-one coaching and grow more time-efficient and profitable models. His group programme is now his biggest earner and has led to him becoming the go-to guy in his gym.

This new success has opened so many doors for Brendon. His latest opportunities have included hiring a new staff member to run another service and speaking at two events. His authority is now growing beyond the city he lives in and he currently coaches clients all over the UK. Brendon recently opened his dream facility and is building the best fitness community in his city. By the time this book is published, I reckon it will already be just that.

Brendon's case exemplifies how powerful raising your authority can be when you challenge the norm and embrace change for personal and business growth.

Summary

- Having authority in your business is so powerful that not only does it give clients a better experience, it makes attracting new ones much easier. This is because existing clients are reassured they are in the right place and prospects already trust you before signing up.

- Improving your authority can start today. Remember, it's conducting yourself better in the gym. It's doing what other PTs aren't prepared to and it's creating demand for your service and classes. This will improve people's perception of your business and they'll take it more seriously.

- Fast-track gaining authority by drawing on the clients that you speak to every day. Reach out to them all and arrange your first event at their workplace.

- Optimise your social media. Go through your profiles and do a self-audit. You could even get a friend or loved one to help. Take notes on how your page looks at first glance, how your bio reads, what your most recent images look like and what impression your display picture creates. What could be improved? Write this down and action it.

- Look at how your prospects can contact you. Is there a clear CTA that urges and directs them to the next stage? How simple is the process? The more confusing and difficult, the fewer enquiries you'll get.

- Check over your pages to ensure that your branding is evident throughout. Let your products and programmes do the talking and people will fully understand the 'why' and the 'how' aspect of your service.

- The most crucial thing to include in your social media profile is a showcase of your results. Make sure it speaks to your niche market to get them interested in signing up to achieve the same for themselves.

- Remember, getting the result is half the job – don't be the world's best-kept secret. Show the world how great a coach you are.

FOUR
Nurture Leads

Time for things to get exciting. In this chapter, we'll explore the value of building relationships and trust with people. We'll look at how we can give value to those who aren't quite ready to sign up for our services and how we can create a pipeline of prospects who will eventually become paying clients.

This chapter will be very tactical, but as I promised at the start of this book, we will keep it jargon-free and straightforward. After reading it, you will be clearer on how to identify the people who are ready to buy and those who need more time.

Coaches often set their businesses up to be a one-way street. They wait for clients to come to them without ever setting up a process that bridges the feast–famine gap of having no enquiries about their services and having many enquiries at once. This leaves you with an opportunity: to provide the bridge and create a never-ending stream of prospects in your client pipeline.

Leads are the lifeblood of your business. They allow you to plan for the future. Knowing that enquiries are guaranteed will enable you to reinvest into the business, build more resources and fulfil the demand. A constant flow of prospects will reassure you that your work is impactful. Your confidence will soar when you realise people are queuing up to work with you. Conversely, a lack of interest in your business will keep you up at night and make you question every decision you've made.

We need a proactive approach for this to work. In this chapter, we'll look at a tried-and-tested system. I'll give you the framework so that you can build your very own pipeline, starting this week.

Before then, we need to identify the different types of prospects you will come across. Not everyone sees the value in investing in their health and fitness. Sad, I know. It's our job to break down the barriers and educate our prospects.

We can do that by giving them something they genuinely need, and that's not free personal training or coaching. It's a tool or resource they can use instantly to improve one (or a few) of their current struggles – something that gets them buying in to you and your business. Something that nurtures them until they finally want to use your service and have you guide them on a life-changing journey.

What is 'nurturing a lead'?

I promised you a jargon-free book, so let's break this down and look at precisely what this means for your business, or I'll run the risk of making it sound like you're watering a plant. Simply put, nurturing a lead is building relationships with potential future clients. A lead is someone who has shown interest in what you have to offer. This might be someone on the gym floor or online looking for some guidance in their fitness journey. They might not be ready to sign up for your services yet, but don't give up there. So many coaches draw the line there – I call this the 'sign up or see ya' mentality.

There are many reasons why someone isn't ready to sign up for your coaching programme: timing, afford-ability, work schedule, low confidence, mental health struggles, etc. These aren't excuses. But sometimes they are used to mask the real reason. Let's face it, your coaching programme can help them create better hab-its, prioritise themselves more, feel more energetic and improve their daily routines, which would result in the above 'objections' being improved by signing up with you. So what's the real reason? Most of the time, it's one of two things – trust and the perception of value.

Trust is what makes people take the leap and sign up with you (we will talk about value a little later on). Remember, when someone hires a coach, they are about to embark on a journey to better themselves, meaning they feel vulnerable and are usually low in confidence. To add to that, they perceive coaches as super fit and intimidating. It's our job to break those barriers down.

Think of your average gym member walking around a busy gym, unsure how to use half the equipment and feeling lost. Imagine walking past them and introducing yourself with, 'Hey, my name is Chris, one of the coaches here. If you need a hand with anything, just let me know.' These are basic customer service skills, but now the member has a name and familiar face they associate with the gym. Similarly, coaches can be guilty of waiting for clients to come to them on social media. Imagine if you reached out to someone commenting on your profile like this: 'Hey, thanks a lot for engaging with my content.' Both examples make you stand out.

Why? Because most coaches don't do it. This might be an ego thing, too proud to make the first move. It might be low confidence – they might be a shy person. That's OK, but running a coaching business isn't just about teaching an exercise and counting reps. It's about building rapport and creating connections with real people. Just like lifting weights, you get better with this stuff over time and practice makes perfect.

We will explore more powerful ways of building rapport and breaking those barriers down, but first, let's look at the biggest problems when it comes to attracting new leads to your business and what to do about them.

Three problems with leads

Problem 1: Lack of likeable leads

As I mentioned earlier, leads are the lifeblood of your business. So what's not to like about them? Well, we are dealing with human beings, after all. You'll hear the term 'tyre kickers'. This describes someone who registers interest in a service with no intention of buying. I'd avoid that phrase when you're just starting, though. That mentality sets up a 'you versus them' scenario. When you're first starting, you will have a prospect literally on the brink of transferring your money only to ghost you moments later. It never stops. But over time, occurrences like this reduce as you build more authority and use processes to filter those people out. (We will cover this further in Chapter 9.)

Remember, your message should be targeted to a specific target market. Market to everyone and you open yourself up to more wrong fits. An ideal lead would be someone who contacts you about your service off the back of a piece of content you put out, perhaps about a client's journey or a story you shared. The best types of response would be, 'That's the exact position I'm in,' or, 'This really hit home for me; I'd love to know more about your services.' This would indicate that the prospect is similar to your current clients. Alternatively they may message you, giving you a bit of background about their journey so far, their current goals and how soon they want to start.

It would be great if everyone wrote messages like the ones above, but they don't. Reaching out to a coach is a huge deal for some people. It can be nerve-racking, so please do your best to alleviate their concerns by making them feel heard and understood. The crucial thing is not to make assumptions after reading their first message that they can't afford your services or will waste your time.

Problem 2: Price-concerned prospects

The most common message you will receive from people enquiring about your service will be some variation of, 'Hey, just looking to find out how much your coaching is?' Sometimes they don't even say hi. In today's online-centric world, people are reactive. You might post a picture of a client result and someone scrolling past will reach out without giving it a thought. If they have commented or sent their enquiry reactively, they might not have thought things through, and the 'I need that now' feeling could wear off, hence why they might not get back to your reply. This can mess with your head a little, as most coaches blame themselves. They think, 'Could I have said something different?' When, in reality, that person wasn't ready to buy.

A price-concerned prospect isn't necessarily a bad thing, though personal training is a luxury. Your health is the most important thing in your life, but that can come from the basics. Coaching isn't necessary to live a healthy lifestyle. Don't go all defensive when you're having these conversations either. People have a right to find out the price.

You will get some people who will shop around. They will message a handful of coaches in their area and go straight to the cheapest one. My advice is don't lower yourself to that. The right people will come to you for the right price. Coaching is a luxury, but you get what you pay for. You can't be the cheapest and the best.

So what's the solution? Well, the key is getting to understand their situation. When someone doesn't want to sign up, more often than not, it's not the price that's stopping them. They don't see enough value in what you have to offer. The more you understand what they're struggling with, the better solution you can offer for them. This creates trust, increases their perceived likelihood of achievement and ultimately makes them take the leap.

Problem 3: Unpredictable numbers of leads

It's rush hour, it's raining and the bus stop you are waiting at is full. You are barely under shelter. The bus everyone is waiting for is fifteen minutes late. Then suddenly, over the hill, you see it. As it gets closer, you see another one right behind it. It's bitter-sweet. You want to get on the bus, but you wouldn't be soaked if the other bus had been on time. This is precisely what it's like when you're waiting for your next lead.

I have to say, though, it's a little more worrying when it's your livelihood that depends on it. Unpredictability in business is expected. But we want to reduce it as much as possible. The actions we take in marketing can influence this. As we discussed before, putting the right message in front of the right people will massively improve your chance of getting consistent leads – and the key word here is *consistent*.

You've heard it before. Great coaches like you preach consistency in fitness until you are blue in the face. Business is no different. Consistently sharing your message, story and programme are key to increasing lead flow. Even if you don't have your programme where you want it to be, even if your knowledge isn't as in-depth as you want it to be, putting out a consistent message will get more people in. They will test your programme, allowing you to make improvements, and you will have access to more clients with different struggles and experiences, thus making you more knowledgeable as a coach. Win–win.

You will go through stages in your business where leads dry up. That's normal. Generally speaking, if it happens more than you'd like, it's probably because of your marketing. Something isn't landing with the people seeing your stuff. It's not connecting with them. Go back to Chapter 2 and audit the last few pieces of content, emails, etc that you've put out. Are they doing enough? Are they speaking the language of your prospect?

Knowing that you can influence prospects to get in touch rather than passively waiting for them to come to you is a powerful shift in approach, and the impact of doing so will skyrocket your confidence.

What makes an A-grade client?

Take a second to think of your current clients. Now think of the ones you love coaching. Why is that? It won't be that they are the most conditioned, the strongest, or even the ones who have had the biggest physical changes. Those are the outcomes of actions. It is more likely something to do with their attitude or personality that you like.

For me, three things make an A-grade client. First, they are **willing to learn.** They don't have to come to you with years of experience. In fact, that can be a hindrance if they've picked up bad habits. But when clients are willing to learn, they will undoubtedly witness faster results. Clients who want to know ask more questions. This allows them to be more autonomous when making exercise and nutrition decisions.

Our ultimate goal as coaches is to give our clients the knowledge and freedom to make their own decisions, but the clients have to meet us halfway. They can do that by having a desire to learn and not relying on being spoon-fed every step of the way.

The second trait is that A-grade clients **share**. Sharing personal stories, struggles and obstacles make a great client and coach relationship. They give the coach a deep understanding of their motivators and why they reached out in the first place.

Third, as a result of the above two, A-grade clients get results. Whether you help clients drop five stone or you put more focus on mental wellness, that's your business. But whatever you promise the client, that's what you have to deliver on.

This might be an extreme example, but one thing that helped me raise my standards was imagining that a client at any given moment might take me to court because I never got them a result. What would the judge rule upon reading the evidence? Did I have solid evidence proving I did enough for that client?

Did I give them the tools, resources and support to help them achieve the result? If so, great. But if they didn't get the results they wanted, it wouldn't have been the client's fault. As coaches, we need to be flexible in our approach to ensure that we eventually get the client there no matter what. It doesn't help to say, 'You never stuck to the plan.'

That said, clients who get the results they set out for must be shouted about from the rooftops. Not least because it proves that what you do works, but because they deserve every bit of credit for their hard work and dedication. When you find clients who are coachable and willing to learn, the results will almost certainly follow. Identify the A-graders and bend over backwards for them.

Now let's look at one of the most reliable sources for attracting and securing clients.

Structuring a lead magnet

A lead magnet is a marketing term for a free item or service that is given away to gather contact details, for example, workout plans, calorie guides, cheat sheets, newsletters and free consultations. The goal is to exchange the item for contact information so you can engage with potential new customers. The aim is that either they become a client or the lead magnet nurtures them along the buying process (more on that later).

There are a lot of mistakes I've seen fitness business owners make when it comes to launching a lead magnet. The framework I'm about to give you will help you avoid all of the most common mistakes. But before I dive into that, one central point to make is that the lead magnet must solve a problem, especially one that your target market has. Remember the issues we listed in Chapter 2? Your lead magnet must fix at least one of those problems, not only to make it worthwhile, but to make people want it.

Structuring a great lead magnet comes down to the acronym SAGE: It must be Short, Actionable, Goal-Orientated and Easy. Let's look at each of these criteria in turn:

- **Short.** Make sure your lead magnet is easy to digest. For the most part, it is going to be sent to people who aren't ready to buy from you. This means they aren't willing to invest much time into it. They will run for the hills if you give them a 35-page novel on the top five tips for fat loss. Get to the point and make your content as friction-free as possible. As you build yours, you will start to wonder, 'Is this enough? I feel like it's too basic.' These are normal thoughts. Remember, as soon as you get their email or information, you can follow up with more anyway.

- **Actionable.** Make sure to include tasks, big or small. It could be asking them to complete five workouts in ten days, or asking them to send you a screenshot of the recipe they used from your guide. Whatever it is, it ensures they move forward and are accountable for taking action. It gives them a taste of what being coached by you is like.

- **Goal-orientated.** What is the desired outcome from their receipt of your lead magnet? If they take action, what results do they get? Set them a goal, eg, 'Drop up to 7 lbs of fat by using our social event blueprint.' The goal – dropping up to 7 lbs of fat in this example – should be a want or aspiration of your target market.

- **Easy.** This term is relative to your target market. Too easy, and they won't see value in it. Too hard, and they will disengage. Think about a simple tactic your target market often overlooks. For example, if your target market is busy mums who struggle for time, instead of giving them a five-day training split in the gym, give them the busy mum's time machine in the form of a daily planner, one centred around the school run, ensuring they focus on steps, short, effective workouts and set non-negotiables. Those things are easy to implement.

Now you know the what, why and how behind building a great lead magnet, it's time to build yours. You'll be happy to know it won't take long. Using the 'Narrow your niche' notes from Chapter 2, I reckon you can have it completed in around an hour, out to the public in two hours and have new leads in your pipeline by the end of the day. Deal? Great.

For an overview, you can download my Magnet Masterclass from the website.[5]

The pipeline process

Nurturing leads means offering value until your prospects are ready to work with you. Our four-step pipeline process allows you to identify 'now' buyers or 'later' buyers. Let's take a look.

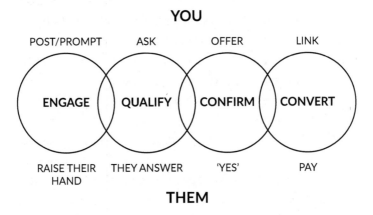

As you can see in the diagram, the pipeline starts with two people: you and the prospect. In the middle, you will see the different stages – Engage, Qualify, Confirm and Convert. Above these are the actions you

---

5   https://chris-bradley.co.uk/resources

should take, and below them are the steps you want your prospect to take. Follow this diagram for every piece of content you put out there. I'll explain below.

First, you post a blog entry, image or video on social media, with the aim to engage the viewer. **Engage** them by instructing them how to take action. It could be asking them to reply with a keyword or getting them to send you their takeaways, essentially getting them to raise their hand. This allows you to take the conversation further.

Next, you ask them a series of questions. We will give you the questions to ask in Chapter 9, but in short, we will ask them about their health and fitness. This allows you to **qualify** them, ie, checking that you can help them and that they want your help (more on this later). At this point, we want them to cooperate and reply.

We then move on to getting them to **confirm** that they would like your help. You can ask this question directly. At the point of their confirmation, depending on the situation, you would either send them a link to book a call and discuss your services further or the link to sign up to your programme. Once they sign up, you **convert** them to a paying customer.

Some prospects will go through the process a few times before they convert, and that's OK. Those are the 'later' buyers. They might not qualify for a particular reason, such as price, time or availability. But remember, don't make the 'sign up or see ya' mistake some coaches do. Keep them in your pipeline and monitor their engagement with you. You may convert them later.

CASE STUDY – CAITLIN

Caitlin was in demand when she came to us for help. By her admission, she was a busy fool. A broken business was even more difficult to run when she had personal issues and health concerns. She started to question her place in the industry. As this went on, her confidence was shattered. Her messaging became inconsistent, which led to a dry-up in leads.

The first step we took to get her back on a path of growth was addressing the confidence and mindset issues. Some of the confidence issues were because of limiting beliefs. She had forgotten her strengths and instead only saw her shortcomings and weaknesses. It wasn't long before we identified her biggest strength: her. She had built a successful business primarily because of her personality and the connections she had made with clients.

Once we reignited that flame, it was time to dial in on her offer and avatar. It was time to upgrade both. She had spent a few years helping clients of similar ages or slightly younger than her. The thing is, Caitlin had already spent thousands on self-development before joining us, so this only added to her maturity. She was ready to serve an older audience. Not by much, but slightly older women who took self-development seriously and demanded more from themselves. Before that, she had clients with less relatable problems and aspirations.

After addressing that, the next action we took was changing her 'sales process' to a 'fit process'. Essentially, we auditioned clients to work with her, not the other way around. We stayed protective about who she let into the business to ensure she was building a tribe of female clients whom she had a passion for helping.

With all these changes, Caitlin now has three to five booked calls per week, a community of more than sixty clients and massive authority in Glasgow as one of the city's top coaches. Her confidence is at an all-time high with A-grade clients on board and a process that gets consistent likeable leads every week.

Summary

- It's hard to turn down business because you don't think the client will be a good fit. But as you grow, your ability to say no will be tested. You can't help everyone, not least because you only have so many hours in the day. But by trying to help everyone, you miss the opportunity to help someone who is a better fit for you.

- Think of the conversations you are having. Are you being too black and white with the process? Are you guilty of taking the 'sign up or see ya' approach with enquiries you're getting? Nurturing leads takes work and time.

- Study your favourite clients to give you a greater insight as to what makes them A-grade. The more you know, the more accurate you can be with your messaging and marketing to attract more clients like them.

- People need to build trust with you to see the value in the prices you charge. This is where vital tools like the pipeline process and SAGE lead magnets come into play. They bridge the gap between someone coming across your profile and becoming a paying client.

- When leads dry up, it's an obvious sign there is a disconnect with your messaging. Speak to your niche audience to ensure you get quality leads consistently coming into your business.

FIVE
Irresistible Offer

What I'm going to teach you in this chapter would've saved me five years of guesswork. This is one of the most tactical chapters of the book. You might have to read it a few times. But it will be worth it.

Your offer is quite simply what you sell, the promise of that offer and the problems it solves. It's the single most important part of your service. Without a clear, irresistible offer that you can articulate, you will not achieve your business goals.

When building my training business, I did the same as everyone else. I provided nutrition and training advice, some mindset stuff and some lifestyle stuff. That's pretty much in a nutshell what most trainers offer. But that's not how you should present it. When prospects ask you what's included in your service and you immediately respond with, 'You get access to an app' or, 'I help you with your nutrition', 'I guide you on what to eat', 'I tell you what workouts to do', you have a problem. We've all said that at some point, but that's just it – everyone's saying it. Your offer sounds the same as everyone else's.

The result? It's harder for you to stand out and get sign-ups. Eventually, it stops you from growing. You struggle to put content out there because your message isn't clear. You haven't built it from the ground up, just built it in the shape that others did. In this chapter, we're going to dive deep into creating something your peers won't have.

You want a unique service that sets you apart, a unique promise that solves a particular set of problems. Remember those problems that we listed in Chapter 2? Yeah. Those are the ones we want to solve with our service.

An irresistible, unique offer makes selling easy. When you speak to a prospect on the gym floor or online and you can articulate that offer clearly, they put their hand up and say, 'Yup. I want to be involved in that. That sounds exactly like something that can solve my problems.'

On top of that, we want to create an offer that allows us to produce content for our programme and outside of it, for our marketing and lead generation strategies. Articulating your offer clearly in your marketing will see your business flourish.

If you ever find yourself saying, 'Yeah, I'll help you with this or help you with that,' and a bit of you dies inside, then this is the chapter for you. We'll build out a service based on what we know our avatar needs. So far, we've fixed your beliefs and we've got you ready to grow. We are starting to establish your authority and we have a system in place for nurturing needs and ensuring that we get A-grade clients signing up to your service. We've also got a lead magnet out there and are using it to collect information from prospects and build trust.

We now have these people in front of you. It's time to present them with your offer. It all starts with a simple framework that grew my business tenfold – the trademark model. Let's get stuck right in.

The trademark model

The trademark model builds your offer, service and programme from scratch, and it starts with a simple triangle.

Lifestyle

The three sides of the triangle are the three elements of your service. You have nutrition support, exercise/ training support and support with lifestyle, environment and mindset, which we'll collect under the term 'lifestyle' for ease.

You build out your unique offer from these three pillars and align your offer with your values, ethics and how you want to run your business for your clients. Let's start with nutrition as an example. We went for 'straightforward nutrition', not only because the word 'straightforward' is inviting to people who are confused about nutrition, but because we wanted to prove that this is exactly what we offer our clients.

To deliver this service, we looked to install a simple approach to nutrition that drowned out the noise. How? By providing our clients with the tools – recipes, food databases, pre-made meal templates, shopping lists, cooking guides, cooking videos, etc. This made our unique offer clear and relevant to the client.

Let's look at the next pillar, exercise. If you train people who want to lift heavy weights, you could call your offer 'powerful exercise' or 'powerful weight training'. But if you train many individuals who don't like going to the gym and want to focus on running or other elements of fitness, you might call it 'empowered exercise' or 'enjoyable exercise' – whatever your target market, your avatar and your clients can relate to.

Let's build out a detailed example for 'empowered weight training'. Your client wants to feel empowered by their weight training, so you'd give them the tools to do this. You could create some pre-recorded exercise tutorials, which your client can watch before going to the gym. Or you could make a PDF resource, such as a guide to the gym or how to use specific pieces of equipment. They'd then have the empowerment and confidence to complete their workouts. When someone is confident, they take action and the outcome tends to be enjoyment.

Let's look at the third pillar, lifestyle. Clients often have the misconception that they'll have to lead a restrictive, dull lifestyle if they want to improve their health and fitness. We know that isn't true, so we'll create an offer such as 'enjoyable lifestyle', to deliver a significant promise to our clients that they will enjoy their new lifestyle changes. You can set up your offer for this pillar in a way that quickly helps your clients navigate everyday life and make them feel in complete control whenever there are events, meals out and parties. Most people think their diet is over as soon as they don't eat plain chicken and rice. Not on our watch.

Your client's lifestyle also includes their habits and routines. Maybe they don't plan their days, which means they fall short in going to the gym consistently. Perhaps that's why they don't take a break from their desk at work. Maybe they snack at night because they haven't prepared their food for the day. We can give them the tools and resources to solve those problems, such as providing a daily planner for them to fill in to ensure that they stick to their non-negotiables for the day. You can encourage them to use a habit tracker to build up healthy habits. For example, when they have their morning coffee, perhaps they could have a pint of water before they have that coffee. Then you've got a hydrated client and a client who hasn't had to sacrifice their precious caffeine hit.

I'm now going to give you an insight into The Glasgow PT coaching model for inspiration. We built our offer with a target market of females aged twenty to forty, having first assessed their frustrations, fears, their wants and aspirations.

The Glasgow PT coaching model

We have spent six years building and evolving this model and have got incredible results for women across the UK, and we're incredibly proud of it. Use it as a springboard to create your own model based on your values, your mission and what your clients need most. And I want you to make me a promise – that you will not try and make your offer perfect on the first try. You're likely to get to a point where you're thinking, 'Oh, I don't know if I can stick to this, I'm not sure it's going to suit everyone.' Relax, it will evolve over time.

We just want to create the first draft of your offer together – deal?

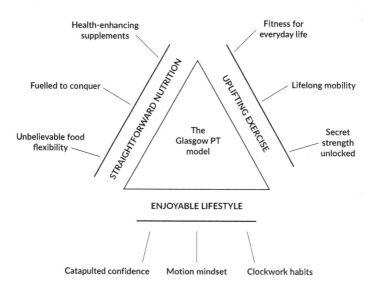

The Glasgow PT model operates on the three pillars of **straightforward nutrition, uplifting exercise** and **enjoyable lifestyle**. Each of these has three sub-pillars. Let's look at these in more detail so that you can see the thinking behind each main pillar.

The first sub-pillar under **straightforward nutrition** is **unbelievable food flexibility**. We make a promise to our clients that they can be flexible with their nutrition plans that we give them, and we're adding in the idea of 'unbelievable' because most people think they have to restrict themselves when it comes to making positive dietary choices. We want our clients to be shocked that they're able to have this food while on a so-called diet.

We provide this by asking our clients their favourite foods when they join and build a nutrition approach around that. They might say pizza, burgers or chips, which we include – within reason of course. We create shopping lists and food databases. And now from having one pillar, we're building out a full nutrition service, which helps us stand out from the crowd.

Next, we move to **fuelled to conquer**. We're going to give our clients the nutritional advice that fuels them to conquer their workouts, their day and their life. It may sound a bit dramatic, but if we get this right, we have clients who are building muscle, happy, energy rich and striving to be better every day. Nutrition has that powerful a role in their fitness journey.

How are we providing the tools for our clients to be fuelled to conquer? We educate them about the importance of pre- and post-workout nutrition. When pre-workout nutrition is optimal, performance will increase, they'll lift heavier weights and recover more quickly, building more muscle as a result. Not only that but if they wake up and have a healthy breakfast at the correct time, they start their working day off well. Increased productivity levels and decision-making capability at work put them in line for promotion, and suddenly, the word 'conquer' makes sense.

Third we have **health-enhancing supplements**. The supplement industry is a billion-dollar industry, so you can imagine how much noise and uncertainty is out there for the consumer. When they come to us, they may have tried a bunch of different supplements in the past. We go back to the overarching pillar of 'straightforward nutrition'. We want to tell our clients to only take the health-enhancing options. When they sign up, they get a list of the ones we recommend, and we explain why we recommend those supplements. We can tailor this to the individual too. We may have a client who has low blood pressure, another with high blood pressure, or another who's anaemic. Our considerations have to be made based on the client's specific requirements.

Now we're moving over to **uplifting exercise**, where one of the big promises we make is **fitness for everyday life**. This means our clients aren't just going to be fit to go to the gym and lift weights, but their improved fitness will carry over into their daily activities. If our client takes their kids to the park, they want to keep up with them and chase them around, so we tailor our service to help them do that. If our service solely focused on weight training, it would fall short of our client's everyday needs and wants. This ties in perfectly with **lifelong mobility**. I've lost count of times clients have come to us with stiff, injured muscles but on the surface they look great. Unfortunately, this catches up with us all, and prevention is better than cure. Being mobile is just as important as being strong.

Secret strength unlocked is one of my favourites. Many people drastically underestimate themselves. There is nothing better as a coach than helping a client achieve feats of strength they never thought possible. Unlocking that strength can be the start of an incredible physical and mental transformation.

The final pillar is **Enjoyable Lifestyle. Catapulted confidence** is the description of taking a client from shy, underconfident and anxious to the polar opposite: standing tall, walking around the gym, shoulders back, chest up, knowing exactly why they are there and what they want to achieve. This transfers over to their career, sex life, clothing choices and much more. I chose the words **'motion mindset'** for a specific reason. I was toying with the idea of saying 'positive mindset', but sometimes things happen that test your positivity. I don't think anyone is positive 24/7 so I prefer to have a mindset that can flow with increased awareness of your feelings and surroundings. After all, there are only so many things in life you can control; for everything else, you move with the changes and deal with them. Too much focus on the highs means a harder fall from the top.

The last piece of the puzzle is **clockwork habits**. One of the biggest reasons people delay starting their fitness journey is thinking they have to become a fitness bunny overnight. Many don't believe they can get instant results just by changing a few habits in their life. The next level is making the good habits clockwork. Predictable, reliable actions that accumulate over time to yield incredible results. These habits are all around you. Every part of your journey becomes easier once they are installed.

That is the Glasgow PT coaching model. Time to make yours, drawing out and thinking about what you want inside your service. After you have the three pillars and nine sub-pillars, keep growing from there, and you'll end up with a comprehensive service that is unique to you and offers way more than check-ins and nutrition plans.

What's your client's dream result?

We've spent some time already assessing your avatar's ideal goal. We've talked about what they want and what they aspire to achieve. These things go into our trademark model to provide the tools for our clients to achieve their dream results.

It's crucial you know your client's dream result because when you fully understand it, you can create a service that provides it. When you do that, incredible things happen because clients immediately buy in to your service.

Take a trip back to the 'narrow your niche' exercise you completed in Chapter 2 and have that handy so that you can build out your client's 'dream result'. What is the dream they would like to achieve? You don't have to have a one-word answer here – think about the end goal for most of your clients and build your service out with that. How would they feel if they achieved that goal? It's often the opposite of how they felt when they first came to you.

Before you go ahead and start to fill in the blanks to create your own model, I want you to go over it in your head. When I was writing this book, I went on many a soul-searching walk, took a lot of notes, crossed some stuff out and then rewrote it. Brainstorming is essential. Let the creative juices flow.

BORE

BORE stands for:

- Brainstorm
- Outline
- Record
- Edit

Just like my process for writing this book, you can use the BORE acronym when building any project for your business. In your case, you **brainstorm** the three pillars, the different categories and topics that make up those pillars, and you end up with nine points. You could add more, but think about where you're at in your business right now. Do you really need that much detail? Are you in a position where you just need to get the dream result nailed, the three pillars, and some extra resources for them? Because that's absolutely fine. As I said, we can add to this as we go.

You have complete freedom here. I like going old school with a pen and notepad and drawing and writing until things flow from my brain to the pen. Whatever brainstorming means for you, whether it's an electronic process, going on a walk, or leaving yourself voice memos, go for that.

Next we move on to the **outline** part. This is straight-forward and can be as simple as scribbling. Draw the triangle and write the three pillars. Never mind fancy names for now, just let your brain guide the pen. You'll have shapes and words, and that's a start.

Nothing is final here. If you start to get overwhelmed, leave it for a bit and return to it later. Whatever you get down is something to edit or something to go off, which will keep momentum going.

After this, we **record** what we've come up with. This could be writing, but you can speak out what you've built so far too. One excellent tip is to record it as if you're explaining it to a group of clients. This could be done over a voice memo or in a presentation style. It doesn't matter how, but the process alone of speaking your ideas out loud helps the brain understand if they actually make sense. Some things on paper look okay, but we start to identify holes in our thinking if we speak it aloud. Listen back to your recording and ask yourself or your significant other if it makes sense. By doing that, it's like editing a first draft. I did the exact same when writing this book. I spoke my ideas out loud and then when it came to writing it, it was much easier because I could fill in the gaps.

Lastly, **edit**. Editing can be done over time, because you will be changing and tweaking your ideas as you go. Usually you have to put your ideas into practice before they make sense. You have to run them by clients to get different opinions, and people have different learning styles, so if you present your ideas in different ways, you'll get further feedback.

Score your current clients

This is the exciting part. We have spoken already about attracting the ideal prospect and finding A-grade clients. Now you're implementing these new ideas, you have the opportunity to audit your current clients. You've spent a lot of time building your pillars and creating your model and now you're going to see where your current clients fit within your new coaching model. This model represents your values, ethics and what you want to provide, and you will have signed clients up before you introduced that, so there will be some clients in your programme who are the wrong fit. You may have already identified that from Chapter 2.

Score your current clients based on how well they fit with your new trademark model. Are they getting the most out of the service? Could they be brought up to the level of the model? We aren't looking for clients to put on the chopping block here. This analysis is to ensure that your service aligns with the clients you've got and that they fit with where you want to take the business.

Not every client has to filter through this, and we can edit our trademark model again. If you find that 80–90% of your current clients that you enjoy training don't fit with your new model, it just means that as you and your business grow, so will the clientele you help. That said, you can't fit square pegs into round holes, so it will be worth having conversations with any clients who really aren't a good fit. This doesn't call for you to start sacking clients, but to have a chat to make sure that you know exactly what the client wants from your service and to be honest with them about whether you can provide that now or not.

Share it, own it

This is my favourite part of the trademark model process. In 2020, when I shared my first ever trademark
model with The Glasgow PT clients, I was in my gym.
We had a 65-inch TV up on the wall, where I presented
my model via video. I explained to my clients, 'This is
the new model. This is how we will deliver our service
to you guys to ensure you get the best possible service
and results. I am accountable for ensuring that I provide everything on the model and if I don't, I would
love to be challenged on it.' This was really powerful.
I got such good buy-in from my clients.

You might not want to deliver your model like this,
but you need to own it and share it in a way that
suits you. You can take the lead and make sure that
any client who has concerns is able to challenge your
ideas constructively. You could say, 'This is what
we offer within the programme. Please let us know
if we let you down, we're in the middle of building
the majority of it, and we can't wait for you to get on
board with it and reap the benefits.' This is important because, quite honestly, when a client doesn't get
results or doesn't adhere, they tend to get the blame.
It's never the coach's fault. It's, 'Yeah, you never stuck
to your calories,' or, 'You never adhered to your training,' when in actual fact, the coaches should be held
accountable for getting the client the result.

It's not good enough to say, 'Yeah, the client never did it.' What you've got to remember is that your model promises to deliver them a dream result. It holds both parties accountable, and there's no hiding for either you or them. This raises the standard of the entire group, you and the clients, and you have a quality service.

When you've brainstormed, outlined, recorded and edited your model, share it with your clients. They will get excited. Bonus points if you go and share it on social media, because I guarantee that other trainers will be jealous, and new prospects will be interested because you've just stood out from the norm. I'd love to hear how it goes down.

CASE STUDY – MAT

Mat runs a large facility in England. He had a bunch of members, but the gym had no real culture to it. There was a lot of random posting, not much business structure and many different types of gym members. This stopped him from producing content in his programme and getting consistent client results.

Mat didn't have an ideal avatar, so within his small personal training group, there would be someone at the age of fifty, someone aged eighteen, men, women, someone who wanted to lift weights, someone who wanted to improve their cardiovascular health, etc. There's nothing wrong with that, but Mat didn't feel he had control over attracting new leads or achieving client fulfilment. It left him burnt out, losing his passion for the job and contemplating whether or not to keep his gym open.

He reached out to us to get that fire back in his belly. We built him a ninety-day plan, with a trademark model we built from the ground up. When we made that, we identified who he loved helping. It was time to dial in on the members that brought a lot to his community. We then shared that trademark model on social media and Mat was unapologetic about this. He showcased it at least twice a month. He had done a lot of work to get it to where it was, so you can bet he was showing it off.

Mat then made training and procedure plans in line with his three pillars. As a result of all this, it reignited the flame inside. His confidence was through the roof. He was back on the gym floor, thriving and loving life. He was showcasing a service with a solution instead of just having members coming in training. There was a clear vehicle for his clients to achieve their dream result.

Mat now has a gym that dominates his area and has never-ending content ideas because he dips back into his trademark model. He's absolutely thriving. He grabbed the trademark model framework by the horns and never looked back.

Summary

- The trademark model is something that can guide the features of your service, your marketing and your sales process. It's that powerful.

- The Glasgow PT model gives you an idea of a fully operational version of a trademark model. It has evolved over time, so don't assume you should have something like that straight away. Get a first draft ready and take it from there.

- Your client's dream result is something that should be hardwired into you. When it's top of mind, it serves as a purpose for everything you do. It keeps everything worthwhile. At the end of the day, what's the point in spending time working on tasks for clients if that isn't going to improve their experience of your service or the results they get?

- The three pillars act as the foundations of your model and represent your vision and values. These should be unique to you. Stand out from the crowd and grow your business. Use sub-pillars to drill down into your specific client offering.

- Develop your model using the BORE framework. This serves as a protector to the perfectionists out there. Don't stare at a piece of paper unsure what to write. Get scribbling. It doesn't have to be right first time.

- As you implement changes in your business, assess your current clients. The more changes you make – even when they're for the better – the more likely you are to cause unrest among your longer-term clients. Most people don't like change. You will be making changes for the majority, though, and will be doing so for the good of your business.

- Shout about your new model from the rooftops. Own it and share the passion and story that went into building it. This serves as great internal marketing for existing clients as well as marketing for your social media channels to attract new prospects.

SIX

Epic Education

It's time to delve deeper into you becoming more than someone who counts reps on the gym floor. Education is something that you should constantly seek to become a better coach, person and role model. How else are you going to educate your clients?

Let me take you back to a story from when I first qualified. I got my certificate, started applying for jobs and got my first job in a gym... and suddenly, I started to worry. Why? Because it didn't feel like I had learned anything. The thought of someone approaching me on the gym floor and asking about training or nutrition worried me. Despite having eight years of customer service, I was in front of people feeling like an imposter. I knew how to train myself and how to eat healthily. But I didn't know how to articulate that to other people. Being faced with this fear emphasised to me how little the personal training course had taught me. It was vital for me to seek further education.

In this chapter, we'll talk about why you don't have to be a scientist. You can use your own techniques, your own cues and your own skill sets to educate your clients. There's no need for you to be reeling off names of muscle groups, bones, ligaments and tendons to them, nor explaining the micronutrients of each food or giving an in-depth analysis of insulin and mitochondria. It's about educating the clients in a way that works for them.

For most coaches, the hardest thing about educating clients is having the confidence to actually do it. You will learn on the job, so be prepared for that. Don't think that after qualifying or even reading this book you'll be ready to take over the world. Just like when you got your driving licence, you don't truly learn how to drive until you're out there doing it by yourself.

The benefits of educating clients

Educating your clients is important because they have to understand why they're doing things. You'd be a pretty bad personal trainer if all you did was bark orders. I'm sorry, but that doesn't cut it anymore. The days of the bootcamp instructor with army clothes shouting, 'Drop and give me twenty' are over. The standard of personal training has reached new heights. Now the job of a personal trainer is to educate clients to make decisions by themselves on things like nutrition, training, lifestyle, habits and routines. Doing so leads them to trust you more and form a better working relationship with you, as you communicate with your client, listen to their unique circumstances and deliver them knowledge and resources. The knock-on effect of this is that you will be able to charge a premium for your service. Your clients will get amazing results and as a result, they'll stick around and attract new clients your way.

When you finish this chapter, don't go away and buy an encyclopaedia. Take time to get your first couple of clients in the door, or to reflect on the current number you have. How much education are you giving them? Is it too little? Is it a lot? A great indicator of this is how often you repeat yourself. If you're constantly saying the same things to the same clients, there's a chance that your education isn't landing – or it's non-existent. If you don't start educating these clients, you can't grow your business as you won't get dream results, just average outcomes. The most obvious benefit of educating clients is achieving better results. They will make better decisions that will accumulate over time so that they'll reach their goals sooner and live a healthier, happier life.

Knowledge is more important than motivation

People often talk about motivation being the single biggest driving force behind clients getting life-changing results. Here's a familiar scenario I saw when I worked in a commercial gym – people would get to the top of the stairs after having fought the temptation to go home and eat junk. They'd had a busy and stressful day at work but they were there with their towel and their water bottle. And then it hit them: 'What now? What do I do?'

That tells you that motivation isn't the primary factor to success because they had got themselves there. Motivation isn't enough. The problem was that they didn't have the knowledge on what to do when they got there. This directly impacted their confidence. With clients like this, if you educate them on exactly how to use the gym and give them a progressive plan with purpose, they will get better each time they go. They'll develop their skills, which will not only encourage them to keep coming back, but will also empower them to feel that they can do more. They'll push themselves. Education creates confidence, which is a powerful tool.

Confidence is key for coaches too. It's all well and good saying that we're going to educate clients but, of course, we need to be confident enough to do that. What most people don't realise is that personal trainers are just human beings with a couple of letters at the end of their name. Quite often, they have loved exercise, have played a sport and have decided to pursue a career in health and fitness. But they might be battling confidence issues, mental health, anxiety, stress, and a six-week qualification doesn't remove all of that.

I see the effects of low confidence on coaches every single week, unfortunately. There are trainers who are great and who really want to grow, but their confidence is letting them down and holding them back. They lack the confidence to put themselves out there, to showcase their knowledge through fear of judgement, often by peers or family members. They care too much about what people think.

Not only does this hold them back from educating their clients, but it prevents them from attracting more prospects. They don't want to post an informative piece of content in case they're corrected by pedantic peers. What then happens is they don't get their message out there. People don't get to meet them, know them, like them or trust them. Ultimately, they don't grow their business.

How to stop giving a f*ck

I'm here to tell you that you have to stop giving a f*ck. To put things into context, I've been doing this for a long time, and the majority of people I spoke to or worked with during the first five years of my business, I no longer speak to. It's not that we've fallen out, it's just what's happened. We don't keep in touch. This tells you that those people who you care about and worry how they'll judge your business probably won't be in your life for long. Although that might seem like a morbid way to look at it, it's the truth. It's like when you had to have the best jacket, the best trainers, the best bag to impress the other kids at school. And now? Those people are no longer in your life.

When I think of not caring what other people think, I look no further than toddlers and old people. Toddlers don't have a filter. They just say what they see. Why? Because life hasn't built them up with insecurities yet. Life hasn't made them want people to like them yet. Sometimes they come out with hilarious comments on the people around them. Then as they get older, they start to care. They develop a filter. They start to know what's perceived to be right and wrong, the stuff you should and shouldn't say.

It's the same with old people. Your gran and grandad literally don't care. They're ruthless, and they too will just say what they see. Why? Because the world's already taken them through a journey. They've got to that stage where they've realised that only a few things truly matter in life. And we're all gonna die at some point. Again, that may be a morbid way to look at it, but it's the truth.

We can take inspiration from the young and the old. Throughout your fitness business journey, you are going to experience the judgement of others. Many coaches hold themselves back purely through fear of this, and it's sad to see. As you look to improve your education and that of your clients, you have to be prepared to stop caring about what people think so much.

Create some FAQ videos

A great starting point for building out your client education offering is to create videos of frequently asked questions, ie, those questions you are most often asked by your clients. By creating FAQs, you can leverage your time and stop repeating yourself. Usually when you answer repeated questions, your answers get watered down over time. We don't want that, because for some clients, it will be the first time they've asked you the question and they deserve a full answer.

We can tie this back to the trademark model. Our first three explanatory videos can tackle FAQs about the three pillars we established. Let's take 'enjoyable lifestyle' as an example. Our promise is to make clients enjoy their everyday life and social events while still being able to reach their goals. How can you educate them on navigating social events while dieting? Create a video answering the question. The next time any client has an event on, they don't have to stress about going off track and ruining their progress. They'll simply watch that video, get the tactics, stay on track, enjoy their event, and you've made dieting enjoyable. Rather than being the personal trainer in the gym who makes their clients feel guilty for socialising, you promote lifestyle enjoyment and give your clients the tools to work around possible obstacles.

We build out our FAQ videos from there. Start with your three-pillar videos and continue to add to those. Common educational video topics include:

- Welcome to the team

- Your training plan explained

- Your nutrition plan explained

- Understanding the check-in process

- How to track your food

- How to meal prep

- Sleep and stress management

- Supplements we recommend

Here is a short framework for creating your education videos. This also works for social media content.

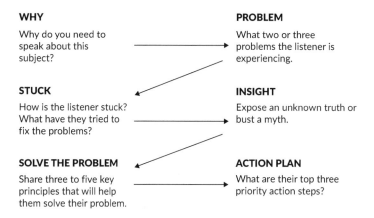

Tell the world

Now you've built an education system around your trademark model that makes your offer irresistible, wouldn't you agree that this is a great time to tell the world? One piece of advice that has stuck with me many years is this: 'Your product is your marketing.' What you deliver to your clients, you have to tell your prospects about. Why? People will want it. They'll want to be involved.

Tell the world on your social media channels what you now offer as education for your clients and why you offer it. You'll be presenting solutions to relatable problems, such as how to enjoy social events while dieting. By having a back-and-forward conversation with your audience about their problems and your solutions, you'll be using your product as your marketing. You'll be giving your ideal prospect a sneak peek of the resources you have to offer. It's a power-ful technique for attracting new clients, and you can repeat this for each pillar of your trademark model and every time you create new educational content for your audience.

CASE STUDY – BECKY

When Becky started working with us, she was a young, recently qualified coach. She had left a job in retail to go all in on personal training. One of Becky's strengths is how effortlessly she builds connections with her clients. But of course, like many newly qualified people, she felt that there was a sudden spotlight on her to prove she wasn't a fraud.

Becky set about running bootcamps and delivering the best service possible. She never did any training or education for her clients. She was still nervous and finding her feet. It wasn't that she didn't have the knowledge; it was to do with confidence. She didn't put educational videos out there through fear of saying something wrong.

When Becky joined us it was clear that speaking to people was one of her strongest skills. Immediately, I knew I had to make sure we harnessed this strength. The first thing we did was arrange monthly events inside her programme, ranging from coffee catch-ups to educational webinars delivered in front of fifteen or more people. I'm delighted to say that this led to her presenting to audiences in person. Becky's even done a couple of speaking gigs, and she now has a client base of more than thirty thriving women.

It's crazy to think that Becky's talents were so hidden. Consistently providing training and educational recordings, combined with her personal obsession with demanding more from herself has led Becky to build an incredible service. She is one of the most impressive young coaches I've met who epitomises epic education.

Summary

- Education is just as important for you as it is for clients. A more informed, knowledgeable coach will be a more articulate communicator and a listener with greater attention to detail. You'll stand out among your peers by developing your knowledge and education skills.

- The more knowledge your client has, the greater their confidence and the longer they'll stay in your programme. They'll also achieve better results sooner.

- Creating FAQ videos for each of your three pillars will start your progress towards making your service better and clients more informed. You will notice this drastically improves client adherence and results.

- You'll also be able to use your educational offering as a marketing tool to cultivate your never-ending pipeline of potential clients, as they'll want in.

- Share your work with the world. There's no use being the best-kept secret. By showcasing what your clients have access to, you'll get more people interested and your business will continue to succeed.

SEVEN
Solid Systems

In today's technology-driven world, almost every business has had to adapt, and that includes fitness businesses. Gone are the days of personal trainers using sheets of paper on a clipboard to document their client's goals and progress. If you catch anyone doing that, please buy them this book.

There are a lot of coaches who fight back against technology, calling themselves 'dinosaurs' or 'technophobes'. I remember having an analogue 'system', tracking my clients' sessions on a small notepad. I wrote their name, their next session date, how many sessions they had used up and the next payment date. There was no backup copy. My whole business was stored on that notepad. It seems ridiculous when I compare that to what I have now.

In this chapter, we will explore the most crucial systems I used in my business to take it from mediocre to one of the leading coaching companies in the country. Systems can be so powerful these days that, when used right, they can save you thousands of pounds. And the great thing is that you don't have to be tech-savvy to install some of them. If you still struggle, you can pay once for someone to set them up then let them run like clockwork. I've lost hours trying to do these things myself, and I'd class myself as having pretty good tech skills. To save yourself hours of frustration, do what you can until you need help.

Innovative and ground-breaking systems tend to be more complicated to set up. I outsource most of my tech work now to ensure I can focus on the job I'm paid for. In this chapter, I won't teach you to become an expert, but I'll explain the benefits that technology can bring to you and your business. The systems I'm going to show you can simply be handed to a tech wizard. Once installed, you will see the benefits straight away.

What is a system?

A system is the framework and process you use to deliver your service. You will have a variety of systems for different parts of your fitness business, from a booking system to a coaching delivery system, to a referral system, etc.

Systems are all around you. What happens when you buy from Amazon? You get a confirmation email of your order. You then get an estimated delivery email followed by a confirmation of delivery email. This isn't anyone at Amazon sending these out, but a system that attaches your name to each email. Amazon isn't a personal coaching service like your business, but their system still makes you feel secure that they are taking care of your order. Imagine if you made a purchase and didn't receive an email – you'd probably get a little worried. Similar systems can be installed in your business, for any stage from client application to your weekly coaching sessions.

When you think of the work you do in your business daily, how much of it is manual? How much of it is repetitive? Could you handle it if you were to get ten new clients signed up tomorrow, or would you be up all night making plans and getting them ready to start? Would the standard of your service suffer as a result? These are the things we have to ask ourselves when it comes to setting up systems. Even if you are just starting out and have time on your hands, you'll still be so bogged down in delivering your service that you wouldn't be able to focus on client acquisition or growth.

You will reach a point in your career when you are in demand, busy and spinning many plates. This is the first milestone, and it's great, until it's not. As I mentioned at the start of this book, burnout isn't fun.

When you get to the stage of working early mornings and late nights, you need to look at the business operations. Why? What got you there won't get you any further. Your earnings will be capped, and with no more hours left in the day, you can't work more and you'll be exhausted. When we look at business operations, we need to deep dive into what you are spending your time doing. Every spare hour you gain from introducing a system will feel precious.

When it comes to installing systems, it can feel like more work. You might be thinking, 'I don't have time to set this up,' but the reality is that feeling stagnant, frustrated and burnt out is worse. And if you're just starting out and you don't have a lot of clients, then even better, because right from the get-go, you can wow your clients without lifting a finger. If you're new, nervous and unsure, you can let systems do a lot of the heavy lifting for you. You just need to achieve a balancing act between making your communication personal but letting the systems complement the personal touches.

Combine the personal with the process

The perfect fitness service makes use of both the personal touch of coaching and the automatic systems that work for you in the background depending on the business need. For example, you don't want a generic system message to welcome a client to your service – that's a conversation that needs to be personal. Conversely, you don't want to manually ask for information at consultation stage when a client could complete that information electronically at their convenience before meeting you.

Picture the scene – a client signs up to your programme off the back of you chatting to them over social media or email. When they fill in your application form and sign up, they get taken to a pre-recorded video of you welcoming them, which gives them their next steps. It could say something like, 'You'll receive your plans in the next twenty-four to forty-eight hours. I can't wait to get started with you.' Next you receive a prompt that they've signed up. You reach out to the person personally with, 'Hey, [name], just to let you know, I'll get to work on your plans in the next twenty-four to forty-eight hours.' Suddenly, the person who's just spent money on your services feels entirely at ease that they've made the right decision. That's just one example of the power of installing a system mixed with the personal touch.

Those who don't have a process in place won't be offering a five-star service. Take the review system, for example. Many businesses ask customers to 'please leave a review', or they say, 'Your opinion is important to us' because they want to know more – they're putting themselves out there for either criticism or praise. Your fitness business shouldn't be any different. We should be willing to hear honest feedback. It's what makes the business better.

As your business grows, you can introduce more advanced systems. For example, when a client signs up for ninety days, you could send them what looks like a personal email at the six-week mark and the ten-week mark. It's not a huge undertaking. All it has to look like is that it's been sent from you. It allows you to check in, but also to serve as a prompt if the client goes quiet. When you have up to twenty, thirty, forty clients, a system like this maintains a personal touchpoint.

Systems also work for you to break through bottle-necks. Imagine that you're working eight hours in the gym with back-to-back clients. You've got a short break for lunch and then your own training, and some client plans to do before they come in. You're flat out. What happens if someone enquires about working with you during that time? If they send you a social media message, what happens? If you don't get to look at it, they get left for hours with no reply. You could lose them as a client altogether.

But if you set up a system where it autoreplies to them with something like, 'Thanks for your enquiry and well done for reaching out – it's often the hardest part. We'll be in touch within the next twenty-four hours. Thank you,' you've got a system working in the background while you're busy with clients, making people feel good that they've filled in a form. That's how a top-quality business should run.

The eight steps of onboarding

OK, now for the fun part, and the part that saves you about three years of guesswork. I'm about to introduce the eight steps that a client takes the minute they sign up with you, in other words, the eight steps of onboarding.

We spoke earlier about client experience being your number-one priority. When someone signs up and pays you money, they immediately second-guess whether or not they made the right decision. They think, 'Is this service going to be worth it? I hope it is.' The eight steps of onboarding are essential to build the trust needed to get your clients incredible results and to work together for years to come. If you and your client have a great first thirty days together, there is no doubt they will stay with you for at least six months.

Before we dive in, it's important to note that these steps must be followed in order so that you can get to know the client before you train them, for safety purposes as well as for the sake of your working relationship. You can't train them before they've completed a consultation form because you won't know about any health concerns or injuries they have. We start with the essentials first and the process develops from there.

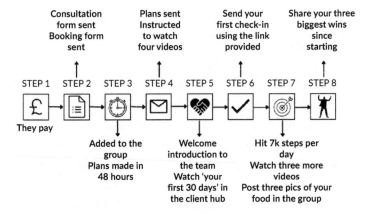

Let's look at each step in further detail.

1. The client pays, whether that's by clicking on a link, buying through your payment gateway or giving you cash.

2. You send them your consultation form. In the past, this would have been done in person with both personal trainer and client sitting at a desk. The personal trainer would have asked consultation-type questions like, 'What do you do for a living? Do you have any past injuries? Are there any health concerns? Do you have any heart conditions?', etc. Nowadays this consultation can be sent to the client electronically as a form. What I love about this is that when they complete it, they can be taken to your booking system. If you're a personal trainer, they can then book their training sessions. If you're an online coach, they

can be directed to your app to sign in and create an account.

3. You add them to the group. Maybe you have a community group that they can be added to, or perhaps they get sent an email automatically saying, 'Hey, great to have you on board. We'd love for you to join our group.' When your new client has just signed up, this is where you have their peak attention. They're itching to get started and receive the goods they've paid for. That's where you can also set the timeframe and let them know they'll hear from you within twenty-four hours with further details, for example, to manage their expectations and deliver on your promise at an early stage.

4. You send the plans, perhaps via a specific app, perhaps a PDF document. This is where the client education system comes in, which we discussed in Chapter 6. You can ask them to watch four or five videos to help them understand the service, get them excited about joining and inform them about their next steps.

5. You give the new client a welcome introduction and introduce them to the rest of the team. You might want to tag them in your community groups, or you could welcome them on your socials. This is where the client fulfilment part really takes off, where you make the person feel valued for signing up with you. They've taken a big step. Sometimes it can be overwhelming, so it can be useful to provide

them with a video here about what to expect in the first thirty days of their work with you.

6. You send them a check-in communication. I'll explain check-ins in detail later, but this is where you would send the first check-in, with a link for it. As I will explain, a check-in link form is similar to a consultation form.

7. You provide more in-depth detail about what you expect from the client regarding the actions they must take to reach their goals. This is going to be client-specific, such as, 'Hit 7,000 steps per day', 'Watch three more educational videos' or 'Post three pictures of your food in the community group'. Tasks like these help clients build the foundations of a healthier life and tackle what most people are neglecting. Think of them as 'If nothing else, do this!' tasks.

8. You ask your clients to share their three biggest wins since starting. By doing this, you receive feedback on what has worked, and they get a confidence boost by seeing that their work is getting results. Win–win.

With these eight steps, we ensure that business operations are in place, clients are receiving precisely what they've paid for, and we're taking them through a warm, personalised and welcoming process. We're also gearing them up for quick results, getting them moving more, working towards targets and introducing them to a community of people who can support them. You might consider adjusting a few steps to suit the type of business you run, but please follow the foundations, because these get excellent results and make clients want to stay for longer.

What are your core activities?

It's challenging to get the right balance between the personal aspects of your service and its automated systems. I've seen some coaches use too many systems and lose the personal touch, making it feel awkward when they're working with a client. You can tell when not much thought has gone into a system and when it's been overused. To strike the right balance, establish the core activities in your business that are non-negotiable for you to do with a client personally. For example, you aren't going to send a robot to count your client's reps or reply to their check-ins. These are the types of things that require a personal touch.

Core Activities = You

1. _____
2. _____
3. _____
4. _____
5. _____

6. _____
7. _____
8. _____

System/outsource

In the core activities diagram, we draw a line separating the core activities we must complete when we work with a client and the other stuff we can either let a system take care of or that can be outsourced.

You can follow this 'core activities' process for different aspects of your business – coaching, content production, or your community delivery, for example. We'll look at your core activities for your client offering to get started.

What are the core activities that you do when working with a client? One fundamental activity is making a client's plan. This is something you would definitely want to create yourself. Why? You want to go the extra mile to incorporate the client's lifestyle into the plan. You can't use an autogenerated template for that.

What else is core for you? Write down all the activities that take place when onboarding a client. Highlight the ones you won't compromise on by passing them off to a machine, another person, or a system. Draw a line when they end. Anything below the line, you want to be looking at leveraging with a system. That's just good business.

What many coaches do is come off a new client call and manually send the link to purchase. The client purchases, and nothing happens. The coach then sends them the consultation form. They then have to wait for the client to get back to them and they send a message like, 'OK, I'll complete that.' The client completes it a day later. The coach then says, 'Hey, thanks for completing that. Here's my booking system. I'd love for you to book in.' Can you see how suddenly a simple process has added layers and time to it just because all the activities are being completed manually?

Analysing your core activities and finding systems for any that fall outside of those can buy you so much time. You'll feel at ease when you know that you're running a structured business, which makes you – and your clients – confident in the service.

Check-ins

Check-ins are when your clients submit a weekly, fortnightly or monthly review of their progress. They offer a chance for the client to give feedback on how their week went, what they achieved, what they struggled with and how they're feeling for the week ahead. In most cases, check-ins address the three pillars of nutrition, training and lifestyle. They also allow you to assess your client's adherence to the agreed plan.

Coaches have put a huge emphasis on check-ins, and to an extent, rightfully so. But they need to remember who they are for. Some coaches think the check-in is for them. It's not. The check-in is for the client, so that they can let you know if there's anything they need help with and anything that isn't working.

Some coaches might be reading this thinking, 'I don't do check-ins. I just speak to my clients.' That's fine. I'm going to explain a more structured way you can do that. But just like anything in this book, you don't have to do it all. I'm just sharing the techniques I've done with hundreds of coaches that have helped. Not everything is going to fit directly in your business.

The purpose of check-ins is to get results. You usually determine these with clients in the consultation stage. Whether it's fitting into their old jeans, preparing for a wedding, improving their performance in sports, or running around the park with their grandkids, they come to you for the result. Your check-ins monitor the progress of working towards that – it's really that simple.

Think about the last couple of months of check-ins with your clients. Has the check-in process been more about them filling out a form for you to complete as a business task, for you to get back to them on? Has it started to become all about you? If so, I've got some questions that can help bring your focus back on the client.

Check-in questions

Hey, welcome! What were your biggest wins from last week?

How well did you adhere to your calorie quota this week?

How well did you adhere to your training plan this week?

How was your sleep quality this week?

How were your stress levels last week?

Is there anything else you are struggling with?

You'll notice that we begin our questions with 'Hey, welcome!' So many coaches overlook the warm greeting. When the client clicks on the link to their check-in form, it's very cold. It's, 'Name, weight, biggest struggle this week?' This can be so disheartening for the client. Those questions go straight for the jugular: 'What happened to your weight? What didn't you get right?' What if the client's feeling rubbish? What if they've not had a great week? Those first few questions are going to feel like you are kicking them while they are down.

Our first order of business would be to ask what their most significant wins were from the previous week. We're trying to change their mindset to make them look for the positive instead of being ready to focus on the negative. If anyone's had a great week, they've got the opportunity to shout about it here.

Next up would be a question where you can ask them about their nutrition. You might have given your client nutrition advice and calorie figures tailored to their goals. You might have given them set macronutrients. Whatever it was, we're asking how well they stuck to it this week.

Then we could ask them to rate their adherence to training. Straightforward, same idea as calories: 'How has your adherence been to the training plan we set out?' Next we move on to sleep quality. We all know how important sleep is to a client's recovery, rest and mood. After that, we ask the client about their mood – how stressed they have been over the past week. We're looking for this over an average of the week. Stress impacts your client's progress, so it's important to address it.

Lastly, you could end with, 'Is there anything else you are struggling with?' It may be something a bit more personal but that's fine, as it allows you to deepen your connection with your client and to respond to any specific concerns they have that you can help with.

These questions are examples – yours should match your business values and ethics and what you want to get from the client. But having these as a template will mean you can tweak the language and tone to suit you. Could you add more questions? Of course you could. But please be aware that we're trying to get relevant information here. Any more questions could result in clients disengaging. It could be overkill.

Remember, too, that the check-in form serves as part of your whole client success system. If they fill it in and it goes well, they get a result. This process is just one of several systems you can install in your business to ensure success for your clients.

How frequently should you have check-ins?

Some coaches believe check-ins to be the be-all and end-all of the service. They think that if they do a daily check-in, or one every other day, they're going to increase client adherence. This is not the case. As with other aspects of your business, you need to design your check-ins around the type of clients you have in front of you.

Why? Because certain types of clients aren't going to need weekly check-ins. With bodybuilders, for example, the most significant thing to check in with them about isn't whether they're adhering to the nutrition and training plans. Adherence is rarely in question. They're looking to change their physical appearance, so their check-ins will be about training performance and enhancing muscle development in specific areas of their body. If your clients are all about achieving world-class transformation, you'll probably want pictures taken to review.

On the opposite side of the scale, there will be coaching businesses and clients who aren't measuring their progress with physical metrics such as building muscle or changing shape. Their concerns might be to do with mindset, mental health, routines, habits and lifestyle. Perhaps a longer-term check-in would work better here to give them time to feel the benefits of their changes. Can you see how you need to make your check-ins work for you, your service and your clients? The middle ground is where our coaching service lies. We had female clients looking to build muscle and change their shape, so it made sense for us to see their shape and monitor fat loss. We opted to receive photos from them every two weeks and have check-ins every week. The photos worked well as a marketing tool, too, as new clients would sign up based on the results they saw in other clients' pictures.

Beware of having too many check-ins and overburdening your clients. If you've got clients coming in person, one-to-one, and you see them two or three times a week, it doesn't make sense to check in with them weekly. It's up to you – it's your business. But clients are busy. When you do a review, you're asking them to take time out of their week to feed back to you the information. You could argue that if they want results, they have to tell you how their week has gone, but you do have to think about what's fair. You've got to remember that on top of their own job, a busy life, looking after children, etc, sending you updates or coming for extra meetings can be a lot to ask.

I was very check-in focused in the past. I wanted to get great results for people, and I always felt that the more touchpoints we had and the more time I had in front of them, the more results I would achieve for them, which wasn't the case.

Be open to changing the frequency of your check-ins. Your schedule doesn't have to be set in stone. In fact, it should evolve along with your business and your growth as a business owner and coach.

The traffic light system

The traffic light system allows you to make sure clients are adhering to their plans, as well as ensuring that you are giving them enough support. It offers you a way to determine where you can focus your efforts so that you can work smarter, not harder.

When you look at your clients for the week ahead, you'll see a mix of those who are thriving and those who are struggling. It wouldn't make sense for you to message every single one. How can you channel your energy into helping the clients who most need you? You look for signals.

There are specific signals you can look for when you're coaching. For example, have you ever had the feeling a client has been quiet and you know they've got a problem or they might leave? You develop a coach's intuition and you'll become almost psychic over the years. But we can't rely on that alone; we've got to look at the facts and metrics.

This is where the simple traffic light system comes in. Let's take a look at it in detail.

- **Red** – The client hasn't checked in a few times, hasn't engaged in the community and needs a chat.

- **Amber** – The client has expressed a few challenges, such as a busy work schedule, struggling with time management, nutrition adherence, etc.

- **Green** – The client is seeing progress, motivating other community members and is enjoying the service.

This system allows you to categorise your clients so that you can prioritise which ones to work with more closely. If you do your check-ins at the weekend, for example, speak to all your clients, assess their progress and give them clear next steps, you can assign them to one of the three categories of red, amber or green. I do not recommend you call a client red, amber or green to their face. I would just use this model in the back end of your system so that you can manage your client base and workload accordingly.

We can see that 'green' clients are doing well. So if one of them checks in on a Saturday and gives you all their great news, it would be overkill to message them on a Monday with, 'Hey, how are you? Do you need help?' They will ultimately not need to be spoken to for the full week, but you'll have other touchpoints with them, such as posts in your community group and checking up on their training on the app. Meanwhile, you need to have a plan for your 'red' clients which goes beyond reaching out to them at the start of next week. You need to drop them a voice note, phone them or message them, pronto. Don't just sit there thinking, 'Yeah, that client's disengaged.' You're the coach. Take ownership.

For any client who is amber, I recommend reaching out to them on a Wednesday. Amber clients have a few challenges and consistent problems, so we don't leave it a whole week till we speak to them again. We talk to them midweek and say, 'Hey, how's your week going so far?' This stops two bad days from turning into seven, and that's powerful.

We've signposted some of your clients who need your attention the most and we've diverted business traffic away from those who won't benefit from it – that's how powerful a traffic light system can be. It avoids constantly being caught up with messages to clients.

TASK: Traffic light challenge

Get a notepad and categorise your current clients. Who would you say is red and disengaged? You're maybe a bit worried about them. They haven't reached out to you or completed any tasks. They haven't been documenting their workouts. Write their names down. Then I want you to think of some amber clients, who have consistent challenges. Maybe they need more attention from you and more accountability from you and the group. Next, write down which clients are green and are winning right now.

Score your current clients using these colours, and then whoever's red, I want you to take action today and contact them. Most coaches would keep messaging into the void. Call them instead – they'll be surprised to have a missed call from you if they don't answer, and that sort of action will take your relationship to the next level. It's not 'you versus them' here. Take ownership and be the leader they need on their side.

CASE STUDY – JARED

Jared had witnessed every stage of success as a personal trainer. His diary was almost full when he came to us. But there was a problem. His service was 100% reliant on him. He pressed every button, booked in his clients manually, answered every message, replied to every email, and so on.

There were only so many hours in the day. As a result, Jared's income became capped, the business didn't grow and he couldn't impact more people. Ironically, most of the things that had got him his initial success

SOLID SYSTEMS

started to be the ones holding him back. The more he hustled, the more exhausted he got, so clients got less of him as he was spread too thin, their results started to dry up and things stagnated.

The first thing we had to address for Jared was time. He wouldn't be able to build the much-needed time-saving systems unless we got him the time to do so. We installed the check-in system mentioned earlier and, on top of the traffic light system, Jared's methodical check-in system shaved off ten hours per week. Once we got the time back, the systems installed were battle-tested and improved upon monthly. Eventually, it was time for Jared to take on new clients because he could handle it without existing clients' experience suffering.

The surprising knock-on effect was how much this improved Jared's belief in the business. As his weeks became less stressful, he saw how far he could take things. The result? He went from making £3.5k a month to exceeding the UK VAT threshold for business income. He takes two days off per week, without fail. His client results are stacking up and with a fully booked one-to-one service and ever-growing small-group personal training service, the sky is the limit. Jared's next goal is to open his own facility. I have no doubt he will achieve this within a matter of months.

Summary

- Setting up systems saves you time and stress. You may have previously labelled yourself as a technophobe, but don't let that hold you back.

- By using the systems set out in this chapter, you will reduce your working hours, get better client results and grow your business. The impact of not setting these systems up can lead to years of overworking. Whatever stage you are at in your career, look to install or improve them as soon as you put this book down.

- The eight steps of onboarding set out a thorough guide to the touchpoints you have with clients as they come into your service. Start with this to analyse where you can implement systems to help you with your business processes.

- The key is to uphold the client experience while letting some tasks go. Use the 'core activities' exercise to help you decide which tasks to keep doing yourself and which to outsource or implement a system for.

- Strike the right balance between personal and automated communication at different stages of your service offer, depending on the needs of your clients and your business.

- You don't have to implement all new systems at once. As you grow your business, you will be met with different challenges. A coach who has four clients won't need as many systems in place as a coach with forty clients. Identify what you can add right now to improve the service and your efficiency.

- It's important to have a check-in process, but make sure your process works for your clients. Use the traffic light system to prioritise communication with the clients who really need it.

EIGHT
Bulletproof Sales Funnel

I'm keeping my promise of removing any jargon that comes with running a fitness business, so let me explain. A sales funnel is the method you use to take a person from seeing your stuff to buying your product or service. Funnels come in various forms – web pages, landing pages and even your communication on the gym floor. Think of a funnel as the journey the customer goes on before buying from you.

One of the most surprising things about fitness business owners is that they expect clients to come to them. They don't have a process set up to attract new clients. They sit and wait on social media for people to send them a message. They'll reply and then wait some more to see whether or not the person's going to sign up. This approach can work to a certain degree, but it's not exactly a bulletproof strategy. Remember the 'sign up or see ya' mentality? There comes a point where you have to do more.

In this chapter, we're going to discuss the different stages of the funnel, how to build trust and how to make someone feel welcome when they enter your sales funnel. We'll take a further look at how to build authority, how to showcase excellent results and how to plaster your clients' successes all over your sales funnel, whatever medium you use. We'll take a deep dive into tracking the leads that enter your funnel.

The four pillars of building trust

You might have heard the old marketing concept of KLT – know, like and trust. The idea is that when someone knows you, likes you and trusts you, they become a paying client. There is a lot of truth to this, but sometimes even those three things aren't enough. Your potential customer might know, like and trust many other personal trainers. They could go to your classes at the gym, but they could attend different classes and see other personal trainers who could say hi to them or even offer them help. They know them, like them and trust them as much as they do you.

Let's think about social media for a moment. Perhaps you're one of those coaches who doesn't post as often as they should through fear of judgement from their peers, family members or friends. They don't get their knowledge out there, and they don't put themselves out there enough. This leads to a disconnect between the coach and the prospect – the potential client doesn't actually know enough about the coach to go through with purchasing their service.

Sometimes on social media, coaches are too focused on pushing their own physique, their own training and their own life that they forget to give a well-rounded picture of who they are. There's a place right in the middle where you want to be, where you showcase your personal life, your personality, your quirks, your traits, what you like, what you dislike *and* you motivate, inspire and educate your audience. If you can be in that middle spot, that's when people get to know you. They get a sense of your character and you prove you know what you're doing by providing evidence of your work.

I've spoken previously about how to not care about what people think of you. But you do want people who are like you to like you. Bear in mind that you will only attract the people you want to bring in to your business if you show the real you. If you are fake on social media and talk a certain way to fit in, you'll attract people who act that way. Some coaches are scared to share that they drink alcohol or have a weakness for chocolate because it goes against the grain of being a PT, but they forget that being a robot PT is not relatable to their target market. Share your experiences honestly and people will connect with that.

Please don't be someone else. Be yourself. When you put that out to the world, you'll attract people who are drawn to the real you and the way you act. I hate to use this term, but your vibe attracts your tribe. It's true. People will be drawn to the message you put out there, your ethics, your values, the way you speak and the morals you stand for.

Building trust with your prospective clients is vital, and there are four pillars of building trust that are essential to the success of your sales funnel. These are:

- Welcome

- Authority pics

- Results

- Testimonials

Let's take a look at each of these in more detail.

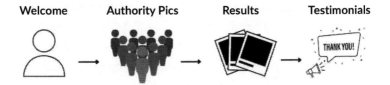

Pillar 1: Welcome

This is where you welcome someone onto your page, whether that's your website, sales page or your social media profile. Have a clear welcome that states your name, who you help and a little bit about yourself. If you have space, you can talk more about you, your journey, how you got to where you are now, your training history, your career – anything that you feel is going to show the real you.

I regularly receive feedback along the lines of 'You're relatable,' 'I resonate a lot with you,' and 'I feel like your content is speaking to me.' People sign up with me because they know me. How? Because I told them my story. Why do they like me? Because I act a certain way, and I do so authentically. For every ten people drawn to me acting like that, I likely put ten people off, but that doesn't matter. It's the ones who are there who count.

On web pages, make sure to have a professional photo of yourself with a big smile and your arms folded. The rise of online coaching has meant that many coaches don't actually get to meet their clients, but until we can arrange client events, you at least want to have your face present across your social media platforms and inside your programme.

Pillar 2: Authority pictures

Authority pictures allow your prospects to see you in a position of authority. This could be a picture of you training or educating clients or showing off your branding and products. Maybe you've put on a lifting seminar and invited a photographer along to take photos of you delivering it – this is a great idea for content. I remember the first authority pictures that I got. I decided I wanted to start doing things other personal trainers weren't doing, so I booked a talk with a local business to speak to their colleagues about health and fitness. And that was priority number one – giving value, having a great time. But priority number two was to improve my marketing, so I insisted we documented the talk. Remember, your product is your marketing. The work's all done, you just have to showcase it.

For your authority photos, hire a photographer. Quality professional shots last forever, they're evergreen and you can use them for multiple purposes. This is what I did at the talk I delivered, with great impact. Suddenly, the people watching my work started to take me more seriously. I was somewhere other than the gym floor, and they wondered why. The talk also bumped up my authority within the industry and local area because people went, 'Oh, he's doing stuff that other people aren't doing.' I seemed like the go-to guy in my area, and clients reached out to me.

These are the types of things that increase your business recognition but also increase your personal brand. Ensure you've got enough authority pictures in the bag to make you stand above the rest like I did.

Pillar 3: Results

When we say results, a lot of people think of transformation photos. Over the years, before and after pictures have taken social media by storm. Social media is a visual platform and people scroll, look at images, see things and react. But this method of tracking results doesn't sit well with a lot of coaches because many don't focus that much on clients' physical changes.

Some clients think they want to be a certain weight, eg, ten stone. We know that's a somewhat arbitrary figure that they were sitting at when they were ten years younger, and if we remove that figure and focus on their general happiness, energy levels and confidence, then that's probably what they want more. Then again, some people genuinely want to change their physique. The rise of mental health awareness has been great, but we can't neglect the fact that people come to us to lose fat.

Everybody's got varying opinions on this, but what I will say for the sake of the funnel and the pillars of trust is that you should showcase the results that you want to show. If your focus is physique development, you will want to use before and after shots, because they showcase fat loss, muscle gain and postural changes.

You might not be into that, in which case it doesn't matter. You can showcase clients on their wedding day. You can showcase an image that captures how your client feels mentally compared to a couple of years ago. Maybe they're wearing the same outfit and they haven't changed massively in terms of the amount of body fat, but they feel like a totally different person in terms of anxiety and confidence.

The main point is this: showcase the results you want to get across. If you post physical transformations, you will attract people who want a physical transformation change. If you preach a wellness approach where you focus on things like yoga, Pilates and self-care, then you are going to attract more people who are interested in that. That's just what happens.

The key here is it doesn't matter which part of the fence you sit on, as long as you showcase results. Demonstrate that the product or service you've got works and gets the desired result your target market is looking for. There's a distinct lack of this in the fitness industry right now. I've watched the progress of mental health awareness and sustainable fat loss come to the forefront. Personal trainers have become much more multidimensional with their coaching now, but they have removed proof of concept, leaving a big gap that we need to address. Whatever your focus is, show that it works.

Pillar 4: Testimonials

Testimonials are some of my favourite things. You may be starting out and wondering how you get them? A simple way is to train some people for free. Have a deadline – don't do it forever. When you're done, get a testimonial from them. Ideally, you'd get it in video format, but it can be a simple text message to start with.

And here is a simple three-question strategy to use to help you get what you need:

1. What was life like before joining us?

2. What's the number-one result you've got from our service?

3. Who would you recommend our service to?

That right there is honestly a one-minute video. And if you can have six, twelve, eighteen, twenty-four short videos on your sales funnel page, they'll do so much to get you sales because they're from real people. That right there is gold dust. Not only that, but it's a great feeling for a client. They get a real sense of achievement and fulfilment from giving you a testimonial because they know they're helping you with your business and they're also documenting a point in their journey that they quite possibly never thought they would get to.

Keep your testimonial-gathering process simple. You can get fancier with this as time progresses. Right now, ask your client to take their phone out and record their answers to those three questions, and you'll build up your library of testimonials. The best time to ask the client for one is when they're just off the back of getting a really good result. If they share a big breakthrough with you, that's when you say, 'Great, I'm so glad to hear that. Do you fancy doing a quick one-minute video testimonial for me?'

You might get some people who are camera shy and might not want to, in which case, ask them to do a written one, for example on Facebook or Google. Either way, you can get either a written or video testimonial from every client you work with.

Pre-qualify your clients

You've built trust, you've got your prospective client through the sales funnel and they're ready to buy. Understandably, you want to make money and it can be tempting to take in everyone who comes to you, but that will do you more harm than good. At this point, take a step back and pre-qualify the prospect to see if you can help them or not.

Typically, you would do this with an enquiry form where you ask a couple of questions that determine what the person needs, what their biggest challenge is right now, and ask about their previous attempts at dieting or training that haven't worked. You can then get some information together for them before you call or meet them on the gym floor. These questions also allow you to decide whether you want to say yes or no to taking them on.

Remember, personal training is *personal*. You're going to be talking with this person frequently if you're going to see them in the gym two, three times a week. Even online, they'll be sending you progress photos, you'll be leaving voice notes, and you'll be connecting with them on a personal level, so it's important that you are a good fit for each other.

Let me tell you a story about when I started The Upgraded Coach. I moved from helping individuals with their fitness to helping personal trainers and online coaches build their businesses. I went from doing something I was great at and well known for to something I was brand new to. I remember taking my first wave of coaches on board and it wasn't until then that I realised I could only help about twenty out of the fifty people there because they were all at varying levels. I didn't have the resources and tools to help that many people at such different stages. I was pulled left, right and centre, bogged down in calls. I couldn't send people videos and resources because there weren't as many as I needed. And when you get to that point, no amount of money and no number of clients can make you feel good, because when wrong fits are in your programme, it leads to people not paying on time and people judging your service in the wrong way without giving constructive feedback. You second-guess if you're good at the job or not and that's a terrible place to be.

Eventually, you'll get to the point where you can be picky about who you take into your service. Honestly, you can get to that stage. You might not think it right now, but you can absolutely have a group of people in front of you who are a perfect match for your vibe. Trust me. It might take a bit of time, but you'll get there.

To assess whether your new prospect is a right fit for your service, you need to ask them some questions, not only about where they're at and what they need, but about whether or not they can afford your offer and whether they're ready to commit. Affordability and commitment are two very important factors. No matter what their struggles are or their reasons for coming to you, you're a business owner and you have to ask them that question, 'Are you in a position to commit to your health and fitness right now?' If the answer is no, then they're not a good fit for you unless you want to dig deeper – maybe it's a priority thing or maybe they're doubting themselves. But generally speaking, if they answer no, then they're not ready to change and you can't help them.

It's the same with the affordability question: 'You do realise that this programme is going to cost somewhere in the region of five to nine pounds per day. Are you OK with that?' If they say no to that, then they can't afford your service. Again, this might be a priority thing where they're spending money on takeaways, or drinking and eating out all the time – and you're not going to tell an adult how to spend their money. But if they're sitting in front of you telling you that they're really depressed and unhappy with their body and they feel terrible, they need to pay to change that, and you have to get money for the value that you're going to provide because it is life-changing.

The pre-qualifying questions

Only complete the form below if you are ready to put yourself first for a change...

Full name*

Phone number*

Email address* [Make sure this integrates with your mailing software]

What's your biggest challenge right now?*

What is your current work situation? (Eg, working from home / office-based; full-time / part-time)*

In twelve months' time, what would you need to have achieved for you to label working with us a success?*

Before people book a call with you or you meet them in a coffee shop or gym, you can ask them these questions to gather information from them and to make sure they're a good fit for you and ready to commit to change.

Tracking leads

There are so many coaches out there looking for new leads and seeking to sign new people up when they've got a terrible sales funnel for managing leads. It's amazing how many leads slip through the cracks, even if you have a virtual assistant managing the process like I do. When a coach signs up with us, the first thing we do is make offers to any old leads. We call it the 'power of three' strategy, where we reach out to three or more people who have enquired about our service in the last four weeks.

But we can only do that because we have a process. Most fitness business owners run their operation on social media, where they get a bunch of personal messages and their peers contact them a lot. Anyone who's a lead gets pushed down the bottom of the pile and on the first of the month, those coaches are back on the hunt for more leads.

Those leads are money in your social media and email inboxes. You need a process in place to prevent them from slipping away. And I'll say it again – it's not 'sign up or see ya'. If they go to sign up but they don't, add them into your pipeline to track those leads. If you can't manage this yourself, you can use customer relationship management tools (CRMs) to keep on top of your sales pipeline.

You have to be patient with people. They might fill in your form and it might not be the right time for them to sign up, but you can't lose those people. Could you reach out to that person again in four weeks' time? Of course you could, and that's exactly why you need to have a system in place so you can keep tabs on this stuff.

You might say, 'Hey, just reaching back out. I spoke to you last month, but maybe it wasn't the right time. Just want to see if you want to chat more about X.' This would be whatever they said on the pre-qualifying form. Maybe they said, 'I'm struggling to manage the kids and make time for workouts.' Insert that, and you've just reached out to someone speaking their language. You never know, they might reply with, 'Actually, I'm ready to dive in now.'

Be honest with yourself. What are you doing with your leads? Is it 'sign up or see ya' or do you have a process where you reach out to them again later?

CASE STUDY – LUCY

Lucy is one of our top-table clients and when she joined us, her only process for getting new clients was that they had to message her first on social media. Her social media presence was good – she was posting consistently, she was likeable, she was getting loads of messages, but she was getting few sign-ups. The reason for this was that there was a disconnect between her and the leads she was generating.

Lucy was putting content out there and attracting people, but they couldn't afford her service. They were low-quality leads. We had to fix it.

What was good was that Lucy had one part in place – she had the likability factor – but she did not have enough authority. We set about building Lucy's sales funnel to attract good fits, to draw in A-grade clients. First, Lucy needed to only get on a call with clients who were ready to commit.

We introduced the pre-qualifying form and simply asked the question, 'Are you ready to commit to your health and fitness?' The yes or no answer was required. If they said no to that question, the online form would end and a text box would appear in its place: 'Really sorry to hear you're not ready to commit to your health and fitness goals. We are super busy right now helping our clients achieve X, Y and Z. Sorry to hear that you're not ready to commit. Please fill in this form again when you're ready to commit to your goals.'

You might think we'd just sent a potential client away, but if they weren't ready, they weren't a quality prospect and Lucy was getting the volume in.

This question about commitment was black and white, straight up. Not only did it deter people who weren't ready to commit, but reiterating the question on the follow-up client call helped Lucy close the sale. Yes, the frequency of enquiries went down, but when the calls did come in, the prospect said yes to the question. Lucy would say, 'Thanks for telling me everything. At the end of the form, I noticed here that you said that you are ready to commit to your health and fitness. Is that correct? Yeah. Perfect. Here's how my programme works. Let's commit.'

As a result of that, Lucy was able to put her price point up. Because the fit was better, the connection with the client was better and she was able to command a higher price for her services. And by only speaking to committed, A-grade people, her call success rate increased to 80% conversion.

As I mentioned earlier, your vibe attracts your tribe. Now Lucy has a tribe of clients who take part, who play the game and engage. What Lucy could have done is not put that question in and carried on taking in the wrong fits. Could she have collected more cash more quickly? Maybe. But she wouldn't have had A-grade clients, they wouldn't have engaged in the community, wouldn't have adhered to the plans and would've stressed Lucy out, dragging her left, right and centre as happened to me at the start of The Upgraded Coach. Lucy's story shows that pre-qualifying can save you so much stress and hassle in the long run.

Summary

- Your sales funnel is the whole process that your prospect goes through to become a client. It's vital that yours stands out and gets the best prospects in. Think of it as a pipeline or the journey your prospect goes on before they become a paying customer.

- You have to take an active role in managing your sales funnel. It is not enough to set up a social media page and wait for customers to come to you. To succeed, you need a bulletproof sales funnel that draws in committed, A-grade clients.

- You may have come across the concept of 'know, like and trust', but you need to do more than simply be known and liked to earn customer trust. For starters, you need to implement the four pillars of building trust. These are: Welcome, Authority Pictures, Results and Testimonials.

- The four pillars of trust check your sales funnel against the following questions: Is your page welcoming? Do you have professional pictures that show you in an authoritative position with your clients? Are you showcasing client results – whatever those look like for you? Do you have video or written testimonials from happy clients recommending your services? Get these right and you'll build enough trust for the prospect that they're ready to sign up to your service.

- At this point, you need to pre-qualify the prospect before you both commit. If they're not a good fit for your business, you don't want them. You're looking for A-grade clients, and you should filter out the enquiries you receive to get the best sign-ups for your business. Use a pre-qualifying form to assess the people coming into your sales funnel before they become a paying client.

- Track your leads. Anyone who shows interest in your business but doesn't sign up may well be interested at a later date. Don't operate your sales funnel with a 'sign up or see ya' mentality. Have a process for chasing old leads – you may convert some of them when they're good and ready.

NINE
Slick Sales

Picture this scene: I've just wrapped up the final notes of a consultation and I'm sitting there waiting alone, my client having disappeared to go to the ATM. It was the first time I'd told a client that they had to buy sessions in bulk, and the cost was £300. Previously I'd charged £140 to £150 and clients had paid monthly on a rolling basis. I was feeling nervous and getting warmer by the second. Were they going to come back?

After five, the client came up the stairs, opened her purse and handed over £300 in cash. I couldn't believe it. I'd actually got £300 cash handed to me from someone who wanted help with their health and fitness. Jackpot! I almost – and I mean almost – said, 'Are you sure?'

You may be wondering why I felt this way. Well, I got into personal training because I loved it. I had a passion for it. When I started, getting paid any more than I was receiving in previous jobs would've been a bonus. As ambitious as I am now, I never felt that I could command that amount of money, nor did I feel that I could make much more than I was already making.

The turning point came for me when I realised that running a fitness business is as much about sales as it is about training. I owned a business, and as a one-person band, all sales were down to me. This is even more relevant now with the prevalence of social media and the number of coaches out there. Building a service isn't enough to ensure your success. You've also got to sell.

Here's an uncomfortable truth: most coaches hate talking about price. They have calls with potential clients and all they think about is when they're going to drop that bomb of the cost of their service. They listen to the client's struggles and their previous diet and training history. They tell them about the programme and how it works. It's finally time to say the price.

When they follow this with, 'Are you interested in signing up?', they are often met with, 'Erm, it's a little outside of my price range,' or, 'I've just got to go and speak to my partner,' or, 'Can I go and think about it for the next couple of days and let you know?' Nine times out of ten, you know you're never going to hear from that person again.

Right now you might not have any sales experience. That's OK. The idea is to make this process slick and comfortable. We want to turn this from a 'sales' process into a 'fit' process, so that it's not about asking the client if they want to sign up, but it's about ensuring that they're a good fit for the programme you're offering. Most importantly, we want prospects to see the value in it and ask, 'When can I start?' If signing them up works for you as well as them, you can go forward and work together.

Sales calls: Be yourself

One thing that I want to point out before we get into the nitty gritty of sales calls is that there is no script and there is no perfect way of converting people. There are tried-and-tested methods, of course, and I'll go into some of them. But it's important that even when you're using a method, you need to be your own unique, genuine self – that's the key to sales success.

When salespeople read off a script, the prospect on the other end can sense it. They don't feel valued or heard and there's an obvious disconnect. The best salespeople put their own personalities into the process. Do not hold back on your personality – nothing bad can ever come from you being yourself, OK?

Yes, sometimes you can change who you are to get a quicker result, but it'll be short-lived if it wasn't achieved with authenticity. You'll constantly try to be this other person, and it's such hard work trying to be something you're not. Use my techniques to complement the way you speak and the way you come across, and you'll have the perfect formula.

The chat flow pyramid

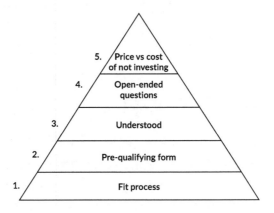

The chat flow pyramid helps you structure your sales calls in five easy steps. Let's take a look at each of these in turn.

Fit process

One of the biggest things that changed the game for me when I was taking sales calls was switching my mindset from 'I have to get this person to buy my thing' to 'Let's find out if this person is a good fit for the programme.' Now, I'm not naive. Some of you might need new clients instantly, and you might be throwing the fit process out the window because you need money and you need bodies in the gym. But please, even if you use the 'fake it till you make it' approach, switch the narrative to 'Let's just see if this is a fit.'

Of course, the 'fit' call *is* still a sales call. You're looking to sign this person up. But by shifting the approach, you go from selling to having a more helpful, empathetic conversation, a 'How can I help you?' chat. The person on the other end relaxes because they don't feel like they're being sold to. They open up and give you information about themselves, such as their problems, to which you reply with your understanding and the solutions you have to help them. Bam – you're selling, and neither of you noticed.

Let me give you an example of two different ways to start a client call:

1. 'Hey, it's Chris. Great to finally speak to you. So glad you booked the call – it's often the hardest part. Thank you very much for showing up on time. The purpose of today's call is to hear a bit more about your journey, find out what exactly you're looking to achieve with your health and fitness over the next three months, and then I'll explain our programme to explore how it can solve your problems and get you to your goals. How does that sound?'

2. 'Hey, it's Chris. Great to finally speak to you. So glad you booked the call – it's often the hardest part. Thank you very much for showing up on time. The purpose of today's call is to see if you would like to sign up for the programme, which I'll discuss shortly. If you want to go ahead, we'll sign you up at the end and get you started on Monday. How does that sound?'

Can you see the difference? The first interaction sets the expectations from the get-go and puts the prospect's mind at ease. We've spoken about the impact of taking wrong fits already, and this approach will identify the good fits for you upfront, before sign-up. A conversation like this also takes the pressure off thinking about dropping the price bomb at some point during the call. You'll get to that bit naturally, after the client has shown commitment and enthusiasm for the service you're offering, as you've tailored the conversation to them throughout. You've built trust and connection with them first, which leads you more seamlessly to closing the deal later.

If you take the more generic sales approach, you stay at the surface-level and don't delve into the client's true reasons for getting in touch with you. If they come inside the programme – which is less likely – you may realise you aren't equipped to help this person. Someone is now inside your programme who isn't a good fit, who's going to disengage and who will make you feel bad about not being able to solve their problems.

You'll doubt yourself and continue the spiral as you won't be able to find your way out of it.

The best way to end a call with the fit process mentality is like this: 'Look, great. I think that based on X, Y, Z [repeating back what they said] we definitely have the programme for you. We've actually got three or four clients similar to you, with similar job roles and similar problems when they started, and they've done exceptionally well. So I think you're a great fit for the programme. We'd love to have you in the community and we'd like to explain more about what we offer. Does that sound cool?'

Pre-qualifying form

As we saw in Chapter 8, the pre-qualifying form is a vital part of the sales process and moves clients from enquiring prospects to paying customers. The form acts as a sort of script for your sales call, but don't get carried away just yet. I've also mentioned that coaches shouldn't read a sales script word for word.

The best 'script' is actually created by the client. It quotes back what the prospect has already said to you in the sections of your pre-qualifying or application form like, 'What's your biggest struggle right now?' or, 'What would you say is the number-one thing stopping you from achieving your goals?' Whatever answers your prospect gives, you can literally say those as your script, eg:

'Hey, I saw here on the form that you said the biggest thing you struggle with in terms of achieving your goals is motivation. Is that right?'

'Yes.'

'Great. Could you tell me a little bit more about that?'

What we've done there is made the person feel heard. We've shown them that we've read their form and we've given them an opportunity to add more context, allowing you to get a deeper understanding into what they meant, what their problems are and whether you'll be able to solve them.

Let's say that your prospect has said that they struggle with motivation. We need to dig deeper to find the real reason for this. After you ask them to tell you more about this, they might say, 'I've had really bad mental health over the last couple of years because of bereavement.' Suddenly it's not about motivation at all – they're just in a bit of a dark place and they need help to get a plan, support and tools to overcome this.

By using your pre-qualifying form, you're finding out relevant facts and developing a specific understanding of the client's needs rather than working on assumptions. Next time you've got a new client call, have your pre-qualifying form in front of you. Go over each section and repeat their wording back, in a conversational way. Say things like, 'Can you give me more details about that?' to get them opening up and building a connection with you. Keeping the focus on them also helps you avoid speaking too much and maintains the conversational flow.

Understood

With a straightforward sales approach, you risk your prospect not feeling understood. Think about it. If you keep pitching to them, it doesn't matter if you're dropping knowledge bombs left, right and centre, they can't tell you more about themselves.

I get it – sometimes you go on a call and the prospect is in a pretty bad place. Maybe they're underconfident, they don't say much or open up much, and they give you yes or no answers. But this is not a reason to take over and dominate the conversation. This is why you've got to probe.

Next time you're on a call, keep listening and ask further questions so that you can fully understand the prospect. At some point during the call, there will be something they say in passing that is the *real* reason they got in touch with you. They might tell you that they stopped going to the gym because they didn't feel confident. They might tell you that they had a kid and just couldn't get back to exercise after having a baby. They might tell you that their snacking is all over the place, or that they are under a lot of pressure at work. That's a lot of problems, but by asking more, we'll find the main problem and the key reason they came to you in the first place.

Open-ended questions

This part of the pyramid is crucial, because if you aren't very experienced with sales, you will ask closed questions, where the only answer the client can give is yes or no. Questions like this have their place at the start and at the end of the call – we've discussed how useful it is to ask a straightforward yes or no question about client commitment, for example. Another good example is 'Are you ready to sign up?' That's when the closed question is most powerful. But if we want to make the rest of the chat flow pyramid work and if we want the prospect to feel understood and heard, then we have to ask open-ended questions through-out the rest of the call.

At the start of this chapter, I said we don't want to just follow a script. However, there are some questions that work really well for the majority of people. These questions typically start with 'how', 'what', 'if' and 'why', and they are asked in a way that invites the prospect to open up. For example:

- Why is it so important for you to take control of your fitness journey?

- What would you say is your biggest priority with your health and fitness right now?

- If you could wave a magic wand, how would your fitness, physique and life look three months from now?

- You can use open-ended questions to follow on from a client's struggle they've shared with you, too. Eg, 'You said you've struggled to work out since having a baby. What are the biggest things stopping you?'

Make sure you continue to ask these types of questions throughout your calls and prospects will give you the information you need. You're going to get a mixture of people – some won't stop talking and will tell you everything, which is great. Your job with them is to make sure the chat is flowing and the discussions are relevant. The good thing about them oversharing is you don't have to ask many more open-ended questions to find out what you need to know. Once you've got that crucial piece of information from them, you can afford to ask some yes or no questions to move you closer to ending the conversation.

Price vs the cost of not investing

This final step of the chat flow pyramid represents another massive mindset shift that probably took me six years to realise. When someone doesn't sign up with you due to finances, most of the time they actually do have the money. But they use the excuse of the price because they don't see value in what you have to offer. On a call with you, they make up their mind as to whether they have received enough value from what you are promising for them to believe your service is worth parting with their hard-earned cash for.

This is where you have to revert back to the third step of the chat flow pyramid – 'Understood'. Look at the things they've told you. What have you understood to be true about their journey so far? Let's say they've spent years trying to reach their goals and they still haven't got there. They've told you, 'I've just not really got into it. I've been doing this for two years and I've not really seen any results. I've been up and down.'

This gives you the perfect opportunity to respond with the value of your service that goes beyond the cost. You might say something like, 'Look, I get that it's a big investment, but the reality is you've been trying to achieve this for two years now. What I'm worried about is that you take another two years to get there, and when you think about taking four years to achieve your goal, that's a long time. You can't buy that time back – it's priceless. But you can reduce the guesswork and get to where you need to go by signing up for our programme. So the question I've got for you is this: 'Is £500 pounds worth four years of your life and achieving your dream result?'

When you put it like that, people immediately get thinking about the cost of not investing in their health and fitness over a certain period, which is greater than the price you're charging, and they sign up.

Another cost of not investing can be that they don't resolve their problems or alleviate any pain they're experiencing. This is where you want to target the one major problem they're experiencing, such as a year of feeling self-conscious, having low self-esteem, a lifetime of negative self-talk. Ask them this: 'Are you prepared to spend another year feeling this way? That's the cost of not investing in your health and fitness right now.'

Prospects share deeply personal problems with you, and they come to you for help. Remind them of the knock-on effect of going through a transformational journey. They might go from being someone who couldn't have sex with the lights on due to lack of confidence to an empowered individual who feels great about themselves and wants to put themselves out there. They'll feel able to go for a promotion at work, get it and make more money. Your role is far greater and more impactful than getting them to lift heavier weights in the gym. It's about improving their everyday life, and that's worth more than any monetary amount. You can't put a price on feeling happy and confident in your life.

Suddenly the price of your service stops looking like a cost and starts looking like an essential investment in their personal well-being. This shift in mindset isn't designed to make people feel worse, or to kick them while they're down. You're coming to them from a place of care, one that holds them to a higher standard and challenges their current lifestyle habits – that's what they came to you for, right? To shake things up and make changes.

When they do sign up, they'll be glad they did. We've got clients who think back to the sales call they had – it takes them back to a time when they needed help the most and they're so thankful for it. Going back to the initial conversation is actually a great benchmark when documenting how far a client has come.

Don't coach on your calls

The great thing about growing and developing as a business owner, buying books like this and signing up for mentorships and business development courses is that you become a more confident coach, person, individual and leader too. Amazing! You'll want to keep speaking and make your voice heard. I hope this book has lit a fire in your belly so you continue to do that more – at the right moments of course. The only time I would tell you to calm down a bit would be on a sales call. The single biggest mistake that coaches make on sales calls or during sales meetings with clients is that they coach. Don't coach on your calls.

I used to fight back against this idea because I always felt I wanted to help people. Even if someone was on a call with me and they didn't want to sign up, I would still want them to leave with a bit of knowledge, feeling that I had helped them with their current situation. And yes, it will make someone feel good for a split second if you coach them on that call.

Let me give you an example. You have someone who tends to snack a lot at night, and they tell you on the sales call that it's one of the biggest obstacles stopping them from achieving their goal. You say, 'Look, I think the best thing to do with that is to make sure you're having frequent meals throughout the day. If you get hungrier at night, but you're busy during the day at work, then it's okay just to move your calories to the back end of the day. Maybe you prefer to fast in the morning, which would then allow you to save calories for the later part of the night, meaning you could have a bigger dinner and reduce your chances of snacking later on.'

That right there is a solution to late-night snacking, but you've got a prospect on a call who does not need to know that. This is a sales call, not a consultation. And when you do that kind of coaching on a prospect call, the person actually starts to feel like they've done well. Let me share something important with you – when someone books a call with a coach to get help with their health and fitness, that alone makes them feel good. They're doing something about the things they're struggling with. They come off the call and they go, 'I feel good about that now.' But they haven't done anything. They haven't moved their body or changed anything in their diet. It was just words.

When you hold back on giving coaching advice on a call, it's not that you're hiding all the secrets and the keys to the kingdom. A training plan and nutrition plan means nothing unless they're applied alongside accountability, support and structure, not to mention the fact that they should be tailored to the person. Anybody could find a diet plan and training plan online and follow that without having sought a personal trainer to give them it. What you're doing when you hold back from coaching on calls is that you're guarding your value – if they want your expertise, they need to sign up with you. Then they'll get coaching done properly, continuously and consistently, and they'll be putting into practice what they learn.

Don't make the same mistakes I did. I coached on calls for so long and I always wondered why my conversions went great but weren't leading to sign-ups. I'm not suggesting that you go on a call and when someone asks you something, you don't say a single word. I'm encouraging you to make sure the conversation goes with the flow while sticking to one or two really big problems that the client's suffering with and you home in on them and how you can coach them on it after they sign up, not before.

CASE STUDY – CAT

I first met Cat in the old gym I worked in. She was with another trainer and going through a massive transformational journey. It was amazing to see the changes she made over a short period of time. Her passion for the gym and self-improvement were the biggest driving forces behind her decision to become a coach herself.

Cat's passion was high, but it was still a tough decision moving away from a well-paid job. She wanted to hit the ground running and leave the other job as soon as possible, but the main stumbling block we came across was her ability to close sales. Her approachable personality made it possible for people to be drawn to her classes and enjoy speaking to her. But people weren't signing up to her services and her confidence took a massive dent. She began questioning everything. Cat was wondering if she had made the right choice switching careers.

We took a deep dive into Cat's sales process and found that she wasn't being herself on calls. She found the sales process awkward and as a result, was struggling to build a connection with the person on the other end.

The solution was clear – install the chat flow pyramid with one important spin on it: Cat's personality. As the chat flow pyramid shows, we have criteria to hit to ensure the call is moving forward progressively. But the execution of the call, question style and telephone manner comes from Cat. This gave Cat the freedom to do the call her way while sticking to a planned structure.

The difference in her calls was like night and day, and she reached a close rate of 80%. She's now recruiting to build her community as opposed to signing people up. It's amazing to see how someone can be rewarded so greatly just by putting their own spin on a tried-and-tested tactic.

Summary

- As a business owner, you need to sell your service. Calls with prospects are the way to secure new business. It's daunting, but having a process will help.

- To be slick at sales, you don't have to be a sales machine. You just need a shift in mindset from 'I'm about to sell to this person' to 'I need to make sure I can help this person'. As ever it's about the fit.

- Your sales conversations need to flow. Use the chat flow pyramid to create an effective five-step structure for your call that still allows a natural conversation to develop between you and your client. This will help build trust and prevent your calls from being too 'salesy' and restricted to surface-level conversation.

- The only 'script' you need for your calls is what the client has already told you in their pre-qualifying form. Quote this back to them and ask open-ended questions to get them to tell you more about their problems. Find out the main reason that they got in touch with you and use that to draw the conversation towards closing a deal as you offer them the solution.

- By asking questions and being empathetic, you'll learn so much about your target market and they'll feel really understood, making them more likely to go through with signing up. But if they question the price of your service, remind them of the cost of not investing in their fitness – it's guaranteed to outweigh your service fee.

- No matter how helpful you want to be, don't coach on your sign-up calls – keep your advice back for after they join you. It's where your value lies. Your clients will see this after they've bought in to your offer.

Conclusion

I wrote this book to reduce the guesswork on subjects that coaches often struggle with. The nine chapters contain information I didn't have access to for the best part of three years, but that my teams use right now in three of our business coaching programmes.

Ironically, I'm going to point out a problem with this book: it doesn't mean anything, when its advice is not applied. The difference between successful fitness business owners and those who are stuck isn't their amount of knowledge about nutrition and training. Successful coaches apply the knowledge they learn. Reading this book alone won't make you better at sales, install better systems or laser target your avatar. Those things will only come from doing.

How do you get better at applying the knowledge you learn? Just like your clients, it comes from having three things:

1. **A plan.** One of my old mentors used to talk about 'just in time learning, not just in case.' This means focusing on the things you need most right now and applying them. You don't want unnecessary knowledge 'just in case' it's useful later, or you'll leave yourself overwhelmed and unclear. You need a plan based on where you're at, and you need to put it in place right now.

2. **Tools.** Once you have the plan, you will use the relevant tools to build them into your service – frameworks, systems, automations, service upgrades, marketing and sales processes, etc.

3. **Support.** Even with the best plan and tools at your disposal, sooner or later you are going to require support. You need someone who can act as a mentor, who you can bounce ideas off and in turn receive solid reassurance. Having a mentor you're accountable to can be a powerful driving force when working on tasks and projects outside your comfort zone and it reduces the guesswork.

It took me a while to realise how important those three factors are. Now, if I notice one element is slipping, I go back to the drawing board and assess where I'm going wrong. With these three key elements – a plan, tools and support – you will grow week on week, month on month, year on year.

As your career progresses, you'll find different parts of this book will resonate with you most. Our business is never the finished article. With that in mind, it's important for you to take the part that does hit home right now and run with that. It's as good a place to start as any.

If you've made notes from this book or highlighted key sections, make sure to action them in order of importance. Make a list and get to work on them. And please, let me know how you get on. I'd love to hear from you.

Whether we connect this week, next month or next year, I'm extremely grateful you are here investing in your business and personal development. Thank you so much.

Acknowledgements

I've been looking forward to this part. I saw a Scottish singer recently thanking his fans for helping him reach number one in the charts. He said, 'This goes out to everyone who has supported me, but especially my enemies. May you all perish in flames and know nothing but eternal suffering.' I'm going to be a little more generous.

My fiancée Cheryl was the first reader of the book and she wasn't shy in giving me feedback. I've had a lot of long, stressful days completing the book while growing the business, and without her taking the pressure off other elements in our lives, this book might never have been written. (Pro tip: writing a book or not, always pick your clothes up from the floor!) It won't be long after the release of this book that I get to call this wonderful woman my wife. I'm grateful to have found the woman of my dreams, business partner and best friend to share this crazy thing we call life.

My mum has to be in the acknowledgement section. She will read this book and not understand 99% of it, but it doesn't matter. Without her unwavering support throughout my life, I'd have nothing and be nothing. I definitely inherited a lot of her traits and she gave up her life to give me and my brothers one. I'll be eternally grateful to her for everything she has done for me. Now it's time to repay her and give her the best years of her life.

I've had many colleagues over the years before flying solo. At the first gym I worked in, I made friends for life. My first coach, Bull, and former colleagues Callum and Connor are my best mates and the memories and stories we have wouldn't be allowed in this book. I must also mention my current coach, Andy, as well as Craig, Seb and Drummond. What a buzz working with them was.

I have a small family. It's being extended through marriage in the future. My Auntie Kathleen and Uncle David helped raise me and we spent a lot of time at theirs with my cousins Kirsty and Annette. We could go years without seeing one another and we'd just pick up where we left off. That's what you call family.

Cheryl's mum, Debbie, and her partner, Billy, have also played a huge part over the last few years supporting Cheryl's and my career, from painting and decorating our house and gym to always being our biggest supporters. Cheryl's dad, John, and his partner, Alia, were a driving force in helping us with the gym and just life in general. We honestly feel indestructible with a support network like that. We don't need a lot of people, just the right people.

Lastly, I'd love to thank our beta readers. You were carefully chosen for your honesty and valued opinion. Without it, the book would have missed crucial information.

The Author

Chris Bradley is the founder of The Upgraded Coach, the fastest-growing fitness business mentorship in the UK.

Since 2017, Chris has invested time and money in himself and his business to develop the resources, knowledge and skills to build a world-class organisation. He has helped over 200 fitness coaches transform their businesses, taking their passion to a highly paid and enjoyable profession. His honest and open approach to running a fitness business is a refreshing take on an industry full of jargon and misleading information.

Contact Chris and his team:

✉ theupgradedcoach@gmail.com

🌐 www.chris-bradley.co.uk

🅕 www.facebook.com/theupgradedcoach1

📷 www.instagram.com/thecoachesmentor

Scan the QR code below to go directly to the downloadable resources page on the website.